This book is dedicated to all the volunteers, past and present, who have selflessly given their time to the building and maintenance of the mountain huts in this book — in particular, Malcolm Talbot, Dick Howe, Tim Clinton, John Harrop, Michel Dupuis & Wayne Shackleton.

They have served the Club well...

Mike Mortimer,
President,
The Alpine Club of Canada

At dusk we lolled about the fire, watching the ruddy sunset glow, which suffused the distant summits and filmy clouds above and was painted again in the smoothly speeding waters at our feet. The weariness of the battle was in our bones and the memories of our toils fresh, yet who will deny that such evenings make up for all? Bestowed unexpectedly as a free gift from nature's bounty, they cast a magic spell over whatever of hardship and discouragement has gone before, transmuting all later recollections into the sweetest that one can know.

Howard Palmer
Mountaineering and Exploration in the Selkirks

Cover: Abbot Hut at Sunrise
Frontispiece: Great Cairn-Ben Ferris hut at dusk

Published by The Alpine Club of Canada
Box 8040, Canmore, Alberta
Canada T1W 2T8
email: alpclub@telusplanet.net
website: www.culturenet.ca/acc/
phone: (403)678-3200, fax: (403)678-3224

First Edition Editing: Erin Palmer, Wordworks Communications

Second Edition Editing: Nancy Hansen, Christine Haberl

Illustration: Tami Knight

Design, Production, First Edition: Zac Bolan, zbolan@

Second Edition: digital banff

Printing: McAra Printing, Calgary, Alberta

ISBN 0-920330-32-0

Contents:

The Jasper Area

Huts in the Selkirks

ACC Section Facilities

Disclaimer

This book was produced by the Alpine Club of Canada as part of its mandate for education and mountain safety. The material presented may be incorporated into the reader's working knowledge, but its use is predicated upon the reader's judgement that the material is correct and appropriate in any given situation.

Travelling and recreating in the mountains is an inherently hazardous proposition. The routes described in this book involve travel in hazardous areas and require appropriate skills, equipment and judgement. This book is not an instructional manual nor a substitute in any way for proper knowledge of the areas and the hazards of mountain travel and terrain.

The route descriptions provided are believed to be accurate; however, reliance on them alone to the exclusion of other resources and personal judgement is imprudent, since each situation is unique and your conduct will depend upon the particular circumstances of the situation.

People using this book do so entirely at their own risk and the author and the Alpine Club of Canada disclaim any liability for injury or other damage arising from the use of this book.

In other words, you make your own decisions in the mountains, regardless of what this book says, and we don't encourage anyone to venture into the mountains with this book as a substitute for knowing what they are doing.

Acknowledgements

First and foremost I would like to thank the dedicated members of the past and present ACC Huts Committee and other volunteers who have made the hut system what it is today. The countless hours put into building and maintaining these huts continues to be a true labour of love.

A series of books have preceded and led to this book. In 1982 Bev Bendell compiled information on the huts in the area in ***Mountain Huts and Shelters in the Alberta & Eastern B.C. Ranges;*** in 1984 Murray Toft wrote ***High and Dry;*** and in 1986 Herb and Pat Kariel published ***Alpine Huts in the Rockies, Selkirks and Purcells.*** Many people were involved in the original ***Facilities Directory*** which was published by the ACC in 1992, most importantly Keith Morton, Tony Smith, Mike Mortimer and, again, Bev Bendell. I would like to pass on sincere thanks to all of these people for their dedication and efforts; this book would not have been possible without their work.

A number of people were very helpful in getting information to me for inclusion in this book. Chic Scott, Murray Toft, Bruce Hendricks, Greg Golovach and Roger Laurilla helped me with routes I have not done; Ward and Don at *Canadian* in Golden were very helpful with the helicopter access information, as was Ida Cale at B.C. Parks regarding their huts. Carl Hannigan and Mike Mortimer provided information on the recent history of the huts. Information on the facilities operated by the sections was provided by Ron Royston, Glen Hauser, John Wylie and David Gillespie.

I have received a great deal of assistance in the writing and proof reading of this book from Chic Scott, Lisa Brent, Betty Haberl (my Mom), Leslie DeMarsh, Kevin Lohka, John Harrop, Dan Verrall, Bob Sandford and Mike Mortimer. The final, professional editing was done by Erin Palmer, Wordworks Communications.

The idea for this book was born as an extended pamphlet on the huts and developed into the present book. Zac Bolan not only was involved in publishing the book, but he has also been with me on this project from its inception, pointing me in the right direction on numerous occasions; I can't thank Zac enough.

There are some fabulous photos in this book and, unfortunately I can not take credit for all of them. Some of the people who have helped me out in this department include Doug McConnery, Richard Jagger, David Lavallee, Richard Burton, Pat Morrow, Kevin Lohka, Leslie DeMarsh, Carl Freeman and others. Thanks, all.

Tami Knight did some excellent work drawing the icons and doing more and more stuff as my deadline grew nearer. In a "first idea" she gave me a drawing of a guy on a camel as an icon for hut to hut travel. When I asked her to explain, she said that people who hadn't seen Lawrence of Arabia might not get it (hut! hut! hut!). I saw it, and I still didn't get it, but then I have always had difficulty relating to gifted people.

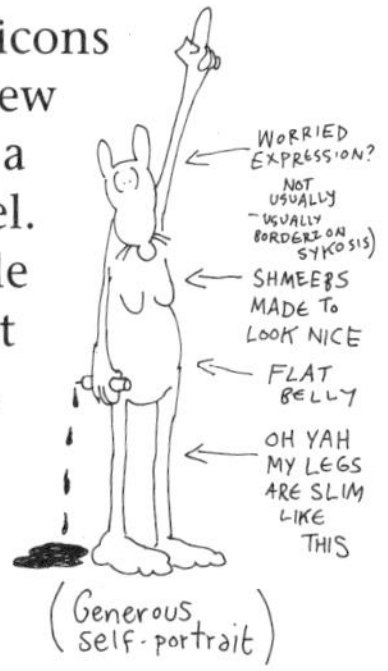

Most sincere thanks go to everyone who has made the journeys to the huts with me, and made them as great a time as they were: Richard Jagger, Gerry Mancini (likely the only person ever to have passed a kidney stone at the Great Cairn-Ben Ferris Hut), Dan, Doug, Jan, Karen, Derek, Leslie, Rob, Steve, Pete (the gang from the Clubhouse), Tony Haberl (my Dad), Richard Burton, Ryan Johnstone and Seymour.

A Note on the Second Edition

The Alpine Club was encouraged to reprint this book following overwhelming response to the first edition. This second edition includes considerable updating of information on the facilites themselves, as well as improved descriptions of access routes and support services.

As was the case with the first edition, many people were involved with this reprint, some of whom deserve particular mention: Bob Sandford, vice president of the Publications Committee of the ACC for his unwavering support of the project; John Harrop, VP Facilities and Andre Kerkovius, VP Environment and Access for their continuing support of all the huts; Peter Fuhrmann for his important advice on history and access to the Rockies Huts; Nancy Hansen and Christine Haberl for their compilation and editing of this edition and, of course, all the volunteers and members of the club, who can rightfully claim complete responsibility for the creation and maintenance of our remarkable system of huts.

Introduction

The purpose of this book is three-fold. First, the book is meant to be a complete guide to the 23 facilities that the Alpine Club is involved with in some way (18 backcountry huts and the Clubhouse operated by the national Club, three facilities operated by sections of the Club, and the Canadian Alpine Centre). As a guide, the book provides general information about the huts, how to get to them, what to expect in the way of pots and pans and dishes once you get there, where to get water, where the grey water goes, etc. There is also information about concerns at specific huts, like how to operate the oil burner at the Grassi Hut, or the coal stoves at Abbot and Fryatt. Want to know where to meet the helicopter for flights into Fairy Meadow? How to change the outhouse barrels? Which hut has running water? Read on.

Second, the book is meant to be a complete reference to other resources that you may need in your travels. There are guide books to the climbing, skiing and hiking in the areas, there are history books which everyone should read, and there are topographical maps which you will need for the trip into hut; this book refers you on to what you need. The access descriptions, along with the topo maps listed should provide you with enough information to navigate to the hut (please read the disclaimer, however). Other references are information resources. Contacts are provided for Parks information and Wardens' offices, avalanche forecasts, helicopter companies, and other huts and hostels which you may want to use.

The final purpose of the book is inspiration. This book won't give you the sensation of joy that comes after the climbs, hikes or ski trips from the huts. It can't pass on the feeling for what it is like to wake up and see the sun on Mt. Sir Sandford or the view from Woolley Shoulder, or to get to Abbot Pass for the first time. That's okay; that's not the idea. The idea is to pass on an awareness that these adventures are out there. I hope that by reading this book, your eyes will be opened as much as mine were by writing it.

If you have any suggestions, corrections, or comments about this book, please pass them on to the facilities staff at the office of the Alpine Club of Canada in Canmore:

phone: (403)678-3200
fax: (403)678-3224
email: alpclub@telusplanet.net

A Message from the Vice President of Facilities

Welcome to the most recent edition of The Alpine Club of Canada's Facilities Directory. This book describes the facilities provided at the huts, gives more detailed access route descriptions than previous editions and includes specific references to recreational opportunities described in other climbing, hiking and skiing guide books.

Since it built its first hut in 1927, The Alpine Club of Canada has been providing shelter and accommodation for mountaineers and others who appreciate and recreate in the mountain environment. The system of huts now operated by the Club's national office totals 18 and spreads throughout the Rockies and Selkirks of Alberta and British Columbia. There are three additional huts operated by local ACC sections in Montreal, Toronto and Vancouver.

The operation and maintenance of these huts is by no means an easy task, and is made possible by a devoted staff and countless hours of volunteer effort by the Huts Operations Committee. The severe and remote locations of the huts (The Neil Colgan Hut, for example, is the highest permanent structure in Canada) can make even the simplest repairs complex and expensive. Keep this in mind when using the huts and if you notice any problems, please let us know. Removal of human waste and the delivery of fuel to those huts with a heating system is also expensive. A portion of your overnight fee goes directly to the Energy, Water and Waste Management Fund which is used to research, develop and implement effective, efficient, economically viable and environmentally friendly means for heating the huts, ensuring clean water and removing human waste.

We strive to provide the best possible experience to our visitors and guests and we welcome any concerns or suggestions that you may have.

Please respect our huts, the other users and our environment. And enjoy your time in the hills.

John Harrop

A Message from the Vice President of Environment and Access

The Alpine Club of Canada is committed to continually improving the environmental performance of our facilities. The club's Energy, Water and Waste Management Committee is an active force in researching and developing various technologies for dealing with backcountry water, waste and energy problems. This research leads us to an ongoing upgrading of our huts.

The club has adopted a **Wilderness Code of Ethics** to deal with the increasing demands on the wilderness and on the club's facilities:

Stewardship of resources and protection of the environment are both essential to preserve the quality of the experiences which we value so highly. As more people take advantage of outdoor recreation, the level of protection must increase or the experience will deteriorate.

All wilderness users have four obligations:

• **Manage Waste**: eliminate adding solid waste to the wilderness by carrying in less, and by carrying out that which you carried in.

• **Tread Lightly**: eliminate all visible signs of passage, and avoid contact with wildlife.

• **Natural and Cultural Resources**: treat protected areas, private property, other cultures and other users with respect.

• **Education/Advocacy**: educate yourself, volunteer your time, and ensure that all who will listen hear what you value in the wilderness.

The costs of conserving local fuel sources, keeping water clean and disposing of waste sensibly are significant. If you fail to pay your hut fees, or otherwise act in an environmentally irresponsible manner, please consider that you are contributing to the destruction of some of the most magnificent natural places on earth.

Enjoy yourself in the wilderness, but protect it for the enjoyment of all, and for its own sake.

Andre Kerkovius

ACC Membership Information

Membership in the Alpine Club

The Alpine Club of Canada is a non-profit, member-driven Club. It is Canada's only national mountaineering organization, and welcomes new members from Canada and abroad who recreate positively in the outdoors. There are no membership prerequisites or requirements, only annual dues. There are various options for membership in the Club depending on your location, your interests and your desired level of involvement in the Club.

Basic Membership

All members of the ACC receive the Gazette, the quarterly newsletter of the Alpine Club, and are entitled to member rates at the Canadian Alpine Centre at Lake Louise, affiliation with the UIAA (the international union of alpine clubs), access to nationally run camps, programs and treks, and comprehensive liability insurance while participating in ACC activities. All ACC memberships are available at family and junior member (under 18 years) rates as well.

Section Affiliation

In addition to the benefits of basic membership in the Club, requesting affiliation with a local section entitles members to the benefits of that particular section. These benefits include access to weekend trips, section training programs, section newsletters and trip schedules, socials and the chance to meet climbing partners. Each section of the Club sets its own schedule of events and its own surcharge on the basic membership rate. The ACC currently has sections in the following areas: Vancouver Island, Vancouver, Whistler, Prince George, Okanagan, Jasper/Hinton, Edmonton, Central Alberta, the Rocky Mountain area, Calgary, Saskatoon, St. Boniface, Winnipeg, Thunder Bay, Toronto, Ottawa and Montreal.

Upgrades to Membership

When joining the ACC you have the option of upgrading your membership to include facilities benefits and/or *The Canadian Alpine Journal*.

Facilities Upgrade

Choosing a facilities upgrade with your membership entitles you to member rates at the Canmore Clubhouse and all ACC back-country facilities. In addition, you are entitled to six month advance booking privileges (non-members and members without this upgrade may book huts up to 30 days in advance) to ensure there is space in your favorite hut. Members of foreign Alpine Clubs with UIAA affiliation need only purchase the facilities upgrade for $22 from The Alpine Club of Canada. These members will receive the same privileges as Alpine Club of Canada members with the facilities upgrade.

Canadian Alpine Journal Upgrade

The *CAJ* has been published annually since 1907 and each year features articles and photos from ACC members on climbing in Canada and climbing by Canadians abroad. ACC members requesting the *CAJ* upgrade receive the Journal annually for a reduced rate from its retail cost.

Group Membership

Larger groups wishing to make facilities reservations may take out a group membership. Group membership in the ACC entitles the members of that group to receive special rates on facility bookings for outings organized and booked by their group.

A Message from the Banff Park Wardens

Voluntary Hazardous Activities Registrations

When you take part in activities which involve risk, you may wish to use the Park safety registration system. This system alerts Parks staff when visitors are overdue and is a local alternative to leaving details of your activities with friends or relatives. Safety registration gives the search and rescue service a time frame for initiating a search, and provides important information about you and your plans.

When you register, it is important that you understand the following points:

- The decision to initiate an emergency response depends upon a number of factors, including an assessment by experienced park personnel of the time it should take to complete the described itinerary. Other factors may include the time of day the party becomes overdue, weather conditions, or the size of the party involved.
- Visitors must be self-reliant. We strongly recommend that all visitors have the equipment and means to survive at least one extra night when undertaking trips into the Park wilderness.
- Once you have completed your trip, you must notify the Park as soon as possible. Either return the registration slip to the information centres or call the 24-hour phone number printed on the slip. Failure to do so can result in an unnecessary and costly search and may result in prosecution. You should make every reasonable attempt to return on time.
- We will check for vehicles to determine if an overdue party has returned from their trip. In order to avoid an unnecessary search, those without a vehicle must surrender a passport or driver's license to the Park offices to ensure that they return.
- Please be aware that registrations are not the same as backcountry use permits which are used to manage backcountry visitor use.

For those who prefer to leave word of their plans with friends or relatives, we suggest the following:

- Leave clear, accurate information and instructions with someone responsible and reliable.

- Tell your contact precisely where you are going, with whom and when you plan to return.
- Be sure to estimate enough time for the trip. A good practice is to factor in a little extra time to avoid false alarms.
- Leave a description of any vehicles used for transport and where they will be parked during the trip.
- Finally, brief your contact carefully on what to do if you fail to return; tell them who to call and when to do so.

Remember – this may be your lifeline. The reporting person who has been properly prepared is an excellent resource for emergency personnel.

National Park Regulations

National Parks

Most of the ACC backcountry facilities lie within, or have access through, National Parks. Access to some huts involves travel through two or more parks. It is imperative that you know the rules of the areas in which you are travelling and staying. Many of the regulations are common from park to park. If you are unfamiliar with the regulations of the park that you are traveling in, stop in at an Information Centre or Warden's Station and talk to the Parks staff about your trip. Some of the major regulations about travelling in the parks are explained below.

Wilderness Passes in National Parks

Banff, Jasper, Kootenay, Yoho and Glacier National Parks collect a fee for backcountry overnight use in the Parks. As of June 1997, the fees are $6 per person per overnight (to a maximum of $30 per trip) or $42 for an annual pass (all prices subject to change). The fees collected from the Wilderness Passes go towards maintaining trails, administering and maintaining backcountry campsites, supplying firewood and removing human waste from the backcountry. As of May, 1996, overnight users of the ACC huts are required to pay this fee.

Backcountry Overnight Use

In the five national parks it is mandatory to register for all backcountry overnight use except when you are staying only at an ACC hut. There is a fee for the use of campgrounds, and there are restrictions on bivouac areas; you must register with the appropriate Park office before your trip.

Voluntary Hazardous Activities Registration

It is recommended that anyone participating in hazardous activities in the backcountry register with the Park Wardens. This registration is free and is the best method of ensuring that someone comes looking for you should the worst happen. Please read the message from the Banff Park Wardens regarding registration, and take the extra time to document your trip with them.

Vehicle Permits

All vehicles stopping in a National Park must have a Park Motor Vehicle Permit. The permits can be purchased annually or daily at most Park gates and Park Visitor Centres.

The huts are located in the National Parks as follows:

Banff National Park
Whyte (Peyto) Hut
Bow Hut
Balfour Hut
Scott Duncan Hut
Abbot Pass Hut
Neil Colgan Hut
Castle Mt. Hut
Canadian Alpine Centre

Jasper National Park
Lloyd MacKay Hut
Wates-Gibson Hut
Mt. Colin Hut
Fryatt Hut

Kootenay National Park
Fay Hut

Yoho National Park
Elizabeth Parker Hut
Stanley Mitchell Hut

Glacier National Park
A.O. Wheeler Hut

Facilities not in National Parks
Lawrence Grassi Hut
Fairy Meadow Hut
Great Cairn-Ben Ferris Hut
Canmore Clubhouse

How to Book the Huts

Reservations are required for all ACC facilities and are made through the national office at the Canmore Clubhouse. The national office hours are 9:00 am to 9:00 pm seven days per week. The office is closed from 1:00 pm to 5:00 pm on Saturdays and Sundays during April, May, October and November.

Making reservations

To reserve a hut, contact us to see if the hut you would like is available; if your schedule is flexible we can almost always accommodate you. Members with "Facilities" and "Complete" upgrades to their memberships can book huts up to six months in advance, non-members can book up to 30 days in advance, and ACC Sections can book up to one year in advance. To reserve these busy huts we recommend the following:

1) Have all the necessary information when you call

Hut bookings are on a computer system which requires specific information to complete the reservation. When phoning to book a hut please have the following handy; it will help us speed up the booking process, and help you spend less time on the phone:

- your ACC membership number (if you are a member)
- the name of the hut or huts you are reserving
- the dates you want to book
- the number of members, non-members and children (under 13) in your party

- the name (and membership numbers, if possible) of other members in the party
- a Visa or Mastercard number to pay for the booking

2) Check back for cancellations

We often get last minute cancellations. However, since we don't have the resources to maintain a waiting list, it's up to you to call back and check.

Booking popular huts

Some huts, like the Elizabeth Parker, Wheeler (in the winter) and Stanley Mitchell (in the summer), are very popular and are booked well ahead of time. Members with the Facilities Upgrade may book huts six months in advance. ACC Sections and the National Office can book huts one year in advance. If you are planning a trip to a popular hut, you should contact the office ahead of your six month time allowance to see if a Section or the National office has booked the hut during the time you are interested in. To make the booking, call back six months to the day before the first night being booked. For example, if you want to book the Elizabeth Parker Hut for August 2 and 3rd, we will accept your booking as our office opens on February 2.

The Fairy Meadow Hut is an extremely popular backcountry ski hut in the winter months. To be fair to all, if more than one party is interested in booking the hut for a particular week, we will collect the party's names until noon on the day that is six months in advance of the first day of the booking, and we will draw a name "from a hat". The party whose name is drawn will get the hut for the week.

Cancelling a booking

We require 48 hours notice (or 14 days; see cancellations policies) to fully refund your fees, but please give us as much notice as possible, as we may be turning people away from the space you've booked. We will accept cancellations left on the after hours answering machine. If you are leaving a cancellation message, please give clear information regarding the name of the party, the hut, the dates cancelled and a phone number where you can be reached. Our staff will confirm the cancellation with you.

ACC Facility Policies:

A little bit about hut fees:

Because of the large area covered and the remoteness of many of our huts, there is a fee for accommodation at all ACC facilities. The fees help pay for maintenance, such as removal of outhouse barrels, supplying firewood, upkeep of stoves, lanterns and other fixtures, and major repairs and additions to the buildings themselves. In addition, substantial contributions from hut revenue go directly into the "Energy, Water and Waste Management Fund" used to develop more efficient and responsible means of managing our presence in the wilderness. Our goal is to come as close as possible to zero impact on the areas in which we operate facilities, and we can only do so with the help of informed and conscientious hut users. Please be responsible about paying your hut fees.

Rates

Refer to the paper insert (p 18) for current rates

Reservation Policy

Reservations are required at all ACC facilities, and are made through the national office in Canmore. Reservations can be made up to six months in advance by ACC members (with Facilities upgrades on their memberships) and up to 30 days in advance by non-members. Full payment is required at the time of booking on a Visa or Mastercard, or with cash or cheque in person.

Cancellations

The ACC national office requires 48 hours notice to cancel or change a booking and issue a full refund. If we receive less than 48 hours notice, the Club will keep a cancellation/change of booking penalty. This penalty is the amount of the first night's accommodation or 50% of the total booking, whichever is larger.

Refunds will be granted in all cases where current conditions render travel to the hut unsafe. Requests for refunds due to inclement weather are generally not granted. All refund requests should be directed to the ACC national office and not to the custodian of the hut.

Large Groups

Groups of eight people or more may delay payment for the full amount of their booking until 14 days prior to the accommodation date. At the time of the booking, we will require a credit card number to hold the booking, and unless we receive a cheque in the meantime, we will process the amount of the booking on the due date. In the event of a cancellation, large groups must provide 14 days notice to the national office in order to receive a full refund.

If we receive less than 14 days notice, a cancellation/change of booking penalty will apply, as above.

Group Members

Group membership in the ACC, and bookings by Group Members should not be confused with bookings for large groups (above); see ACC Membership Information for Group Memberships. Bookings by Group Members are invoiced 14 days prior to accommodation and no refunds are issued after this time.

Exclusive bookings

All ACC facilities are available for exclusive bookings (by both members and non-members). Exclusive bookings are not private use permits, and space is always reserved for ACC custodians. There will be a 10% discount off the total cost of the booking (Fairy Meadow High Season exempt).

Fairy Meadow High Season

From the first Saturday in February to the third Saturday in April, annually, high season policies apply to Fairy Meadow Hut bookings. During this time the following policies apply:

- the rates are different from the low season rates (see the rates sheet insert on page 18)
- during the high season, bookings are made for week-long periods only (Saturday to Saturday), and for full capacity (20) or half capacity (10) of the hut.
- upon booking the hut, the group must pay a $200 deposit. 50% of the remainder of the balance must be paid 60 days prior to the first night of the booking. The remaining balance must be paid 14 days prior to the first night of the booking.

Great Cairn-Ben Ferris Hut

- in the event of a cancellation, groups using the Fairy Meadow Hut must provide 60 days notice to the National Office to receive a full refund. If we receive less than 60 days notice, and do not re-sell the space, the Club will keep a cancellation/change of booking penalty. This penalty is the amount of the first night's accommodation or 50% of the total booking - whichever is the greater. This policy applies to Section bookings as well.
- see the rates insert sheet (p. 18) for current information on the Fairy Meadow High Season rates.

Day use

ACC huts are often used by travellers who do not require overnight accommodation. This type of use is encouraged as long as it does not interfere with guests who have overnight reservations. Those who make extensive use of the facilities (make fires, use stoves and utensils for cooking, dry gear, etc.) are encouraged to pay a day use fee. The day use fee is set at $5 per person. This fee can be paid to the national office or the custodian of the hut.

Emergency use

The primary purpose of any mountain hut is the safety of all mountain travellers. In any and all cases where a dangerous situation could be created by denying anyone access to the hut (such as darkness, stormy weather, poorly equipped or injured individual), the hut users are required to make room for these guests.

HOW TO LIGHT a COAL FIRE
COAL?
HUH?
MY PARENTS HAVE SOME OF HIZ ALBUMS. BUT IT'S ALL ON VYNIL.
1 MAKE SURE ASHES FROM PREVIOUS FIRE ARE GONE. THIS WILL ENSURE A PROPER DRAFT
ASHES TO ASHES
2 TAKE SOME LOOSELY CRUMPLED PAPER.
ROGER! SOMEONE RIPPED MY TOPO OUTTA THE HUT BOOK!
3 COVER PAPER WITH FINE KINDLING IN A "LOGHOUSE" STYLE.
OOH. KIND OF POSTMODERN INFLUENCES...
NO... AND READ ON TO FIND OUT JUST WHY.
4 PUT LITTLE BITS OF COAL ON TOP OF THAT. LIKE, DON'T USE DUST, EH.
5 OPEN THE DRAFT.
CHIMNEY
TOP OF STOVE
HINGE
FIRE BOX DOOR
SIDE OF STOVE
THE DRAFT
STOVE BOTTOM
6 LIGHT 'ER UP! AFTER FIVE TO TEN MINUTES THE SMALL COAL OUGHTOO BE BURNING. PLACE LARGER PIECES Gently ON THE FIRE
ITTY BITTY BITS OF COAL
MORSELS OF COAL
LITTLE COAL HUNKS
SORT OF BIG BUT NOT HUGE
7 KEEP PUTTIN' COAL ON THAT FIRE.
DON'T YOU DARE!
WHUTSA MATTER? YOU AN ANIMAL RIGHTS ACTIVIST?
NAW! SHE LIKES TO PEEL 'EM AN' EAT 'EM RAW!

HORROR-FREE OUTHOUSE BARREL REPLACEMENT PROCEDURE
YOU DO IT!
NO, YOU DO IT
I DID IT LAS' TIME.
IT'S YER TURN
FULL?!
Uh... oh.... really.... ?
The barrel is F-F-FULL?!
1 THE BARREL IS NEARLY FULL. IT'S ABOUT SIX INCHES FROM THE TOP. (read: nearly overflowin')
TIME FOR YOU TO REPLACE IT WITH AN EMPTY BARREL!!
2 COVER THE FULL BARREL WITH THE WOODEN LID ....
Hoooooooo
THAT'S NOT EASY ON THE NOSE!
3 MOVE THE FULL BARREL OUT FROM UNDER THE CHUTE TO THE OUTERMOST LOCATION ON THE DECK.
Hurry Up!
Empty barrels
Full barrels
4 NOW PLACE AN EMPTY, HAPPY, FRESH-AS-A-FLOWER BARREL UNDER THE CHUTE.
I Gotta Go!
5 NOTIFY THE NATIONAL OFFICE OF THE ACC AS TO HOW MANY BARRELS REMAIN.
...so that's how many empty barrels are left an' by the way....
...we scooped you on that new route! an' we had perfect weather too!! Haw Ha
6 THANK YOU SO VERY VERY MUCH FOR DOING THIS!!!
I'm oh so happy Now I got a fresh barrel
Yup, you can believe it...
...I'm happy happy 'cuz all you mountain climbers are so full of sh

Hut System Rules

Please:

- Try to leave the hut in better condition than when you arrived.
- Always fill Coleman stoves and lanterns outside the hut and leave extra fuel outside. Fumes and liquid from white gas containers are poisonous and highly flammable.
- Smoking is not permitted in the huts.
- Dogs are not permitted in the huts.
- Chop wood outside the hut
- Clean Coleman and propane stoves after use.
- Replace the wood you use, including the kindling.
- Carry out garbage which is not burnable and make an effort to carry out garbage left behind by others. Do not dispose of any garbage in the outhouses.
- Take all unused food out with you. Food left behind tends to accumulate because people aren't certain where it came from and it attracts rodents to the hut.
- Empty all water containers and slop buckets before you leave the hut.
- Advise the Club office of any damaged facilities or tools (such as axes and saws) or discharged fire extinguishers. Bring these items out to the Club office, if possible.

Please ensure that you also abide by the following rules of the National Parks:

- Do not cut any local wood for fires or otherwise.
- Do not light any fires except in designated areas.
- Do not remove anything from the park, including plants and rocks. Never feed wildlife.
- Do not leave anything behind – never litter.
- Remain on established trails as much as possible to prevent unnecessary erosion.
- Do not travel in groups larger than 10 in the backcountry.
- Camp only in designated sites.
- Purchase your wilderness pass and carry it with you (*see p.16*).

Best Bets

Office staff field many similar questions about the huts. These are often of the "where can a guy go for the best telemark skiing?" and "which hut can I take my kids to?" variety. This section gives some suggestions for people who know what they want to be doing at the hut, but are not sure which hut would be best for them.

Best Backcountry Skiing

This is one of the most common questions fielded by the staff at the ACC office, and the answer depends on what you want. If you are looking for a place to spend a week, telemarking every day on challenging slopes in the best powder, the answer is the **Fairy Meadow Hut**. The terrain is some of the best at any ACC hut, the snow is great, and the hut is the closest thing the ACC has to a ski lodge (a sauna was installed in 1996!). High season rates apply from February to mid-April, and access is by helicopter.

A close second to the Fairy Meadow Hut, with perhaps more snow, is the **A.O. Wheeler Hut** at Rogers Pass. Here you do not have the restrictions of week-long booking requirements that the Fairy Meadow Hut has, and since the hut is a short ski from the road, so packing in gourmet food is an option.

The **Stanley Mitchell Hut** is a long way into the backcountry in winter, but if you make the journey you will be rewarded with great snow, excellent terrain and a cozy hut. The hut is less popular in the winter months than it is in the summer, and is often empty.

Both the **Elizabeth Parker** and the **Wates-Gibson** Huts are beautiful places to tour in the winter. Some good telemark runs can be found at both locations, but the slopes are not as extensive as at the above huts. The Elizabeth Parker Hut is more accessible in the winter than the Wates-Gibson.

Most Accessible Huts

In the summer months, many hut users look for accessible destinations as bases for hiking trips. These huts are the easiest to access:

The **Wheeler Hut**, the only backcountry hut you can drive to, is without a doubt the most accessible. This is a good place to head to on Friday after work to get a head start on the weekend.

The **Elizabeth Parker Hut** is a mere 15-minute hike from the Lake

O'Hara road where the Parks Canada bus drops you and your pack off (summer months only). The day hiking terrain is unparalleled in the Rockies, but don't expect to be able to enjoy it alone in the summer.

The **Stanley Mitchell Hut** takes about three to four hours to hike to and is a perfect place for a family trip. The trails in the area are fabulous, and the meadow in front of the hut is popular with children.

Less Crowded Options

If access to a hut is not your first concern, and you'd like to get away from it all, you may want to check out the **Wates-Gibson Hut** or the **Fryatt Hut** in Jasper, or the two huts in the northern Selkirks, the **Fairy Meadow** and **Great Cairn-Ben Ferris**.

The approaches to the Wates-Gibson Hut are long (but quite technically easy), and this seems to account for the relatively few people staying there. There are great hiking trails and incredible scenery in both areas.

A party that booked the Fairy Meadow Hut for Thanksgiving one year commented that they were amazed that in a population area of about five million people within a three hour drive, they were the only four who wanted to be in the hut. This is common in the summer months; the Fairy Meadow Hut is definitely one of the best kept secrets in the area.

Look up the word "remote" in the dictionary, and you'll find a picture of the Great Cairn-Ben Ferris Hut. A trip to this hut seldom puts you in contact with other human beings. A one day access is possible, but most parties approach the hut from Fairy Meadow.

Hut to Hut Travel

The ACC huts are primarily in locations which service a specific area; they are not often linked in hut to hut trips. The exception to this, of course, is the system of huts on the Wapta Icefields, Canada's "Haute Route." The **Whyte (Peyto), Bow, Balfour and Scott Duncan** huts are all within about 20 km of each other, and can be linked by standard routes. The Stanley Mitchell Hut can be linked to this system as well, but it is far more common to do so in the winter. Trips between all of these huts involve serious glacier travel.

The **Abbot Pass** can be accessed from an overnight at the Elizabeth Parker Hut, and the Neil Colgan Hut is often accessed via the Fay Hut. It is most common on these trips to travel down the same way you came up.

The **Fairy Meadow Hut to Great Cairn-Ben Ferris Hut** is a classic high level mountain route, and is highly recommended for qualified parties. Check the approach descriptions for full details.

Neil Colgan Hut

Base for Mountaineering

Alpine climbing is done from all of the ACC huts; these are the best, and most popular.

If you are looking to base yourself at a hut and do some climbs, you have a good selection. The **Bow Hut** is a popular base for mountaineering in the summer time, as are the **Neil Colgan** and **Stanley Mitchell Huts**. These huts give access to excellent moderate terrain. The all-time classic alpine climbing hut is the **Abbot Pass Hut**.

Intermediate mountaineering objectives are found at the **Wheeler Hut** in Rogers Pass, the **Fryatt Hut**, the **Great Cairn Hut**, the **Fairy Meadow Hut** and the **Wates-Gibson Hu**t. Harder and easier objectives are available as well, but the best routes are somewhere in-between.

Downright hard alpine routes are found in the vicinity of the **Lloyd MacKay Hut**.

How to use this book

The hut descriptions on the following pages are grouped into general geographic areas for ease of reference and to keep together huts which are generally visited in the same trip. Specific information on each hut is given as follows:

HISTORY

This is a short section on some things which you may want to know (or may not, in which case just skip over it) to make the trip more interesting. It is by no means an exhaustive study of the history of the facilities or the people involved; for that you are directed to the Whyte Museum of the Canadian Rockies, and Herb and Pat Kariel's ***Alpine Huts in the Rockies, Selkirks and Purcells.***

LOCATION

This is the information on where the hut is: grid references, map references, altitude and the like. This section will give you everything you need to find the hut on a map.

ACCESS

"Where shall I begin, please your Majesty?" he asked. "Begin at the beginning" the King said, gravely, "and go on till you come to the end: then stop."

Lewis Caroll, ***Alice's Adventures in Wonderland***

Most of the routes which are used to access the hut are described in this section. Having said that, it is always possible to get somewhere in the mountains from somewhere else, so not every theoretical access is covered. The most common ones are, and most of the huts have two or more options for travel.

Winter access to the huts is not covered in nearly the detail that summer access is, and there are a few reasons for this. Fewer huts are accessible in the winter months, the huts which are accessible have fewer options for access, and, most importantly, most of the winter huts involve more serious travel than this book can prepare people for. To fully describe winter travel to the Wapta huts, for example, it would be necessary to explain snow conditions, winter hazards, glacier travel requirements and gear essentials before getting into the route description itself. This information already exists in Chic Scott's guidebooks ***Ski Trails in the Canadian Rockies*** and ***Summits and Icefields***. It would be unwise to go up on the Icefields and many of the winter access routes without the information in those books, and it would be silly to attempt to put forth that information in this book.

Elevations

For elevation gains and losses, values are given in feet where imperial maps are used (with contour intervals in feet) and in feet and metres where metric maps are used. Elevation gains or pitch lengths are given in metres when there is scrambling or roped climbing involved. Absolute elevations (such as peaks and huts) are given in feet and metres.

Time

Times provided are estimated for travel in good conditions with good visibility. Expect to add to the stated time if you are breaking trail, navigating in poor conditions, travelling with an extra large pack, etc.

Trail Directions

Left and right directions describe features on the approaches assuming you are proceeding in the direction of travel described. This includes the banks of rivers, which are occasionally referred to in other books in terms of "true left" or "true right."

Trailhead

Driving directions are given when the trailhead can not be accessed from highways or major roads directly. All directions begin at a point which is identifiable on a standard road map.

Access Icons

Access icons are in silhouette with an oval border, and should give you a feeling for the type of approach at a glance. These icons are described below.

• ***Hiking Trail (National Park variety)***

This type of approach is characterized by well defined and maintained trails, usually in a National Park. If the trails are steep they are well graded, making them less strenuous, and are seldom washed out or difficult to follow. The Little Yoho Valley Trail to the Stanley Mitchell Hut is a good example of this sort of trail.

- ***Hiking Trail (less developed)***

These trails are either much less developed and maintained than National Park trails, steeper, or both. It is common to have deadfall across trails below treeline, less distinct trails above treeline, and steeper grades overall. Examples of this type of trail are the Swan Creek Access to the Fairy Meadow Hut, and the final scree slope to Abbot Pass.

- ***Steep or Exposed Trails***

These trails have sections which are exposed and airy. You're not likely to fall off such a trail (assuming normal conditions), but the consequences would be serious if you did. These trails are not recommended for hikers with "high anxiety." The Schiesser Ledges to the Neil Colgan Hut, and even some short sections of the Mt. Colin Hut trail would fall into this category.

- ***Scrambling***

This icon denotes a trail which involves hands-on-rock scrambling. It may or may not be accompanied by the exposed trail icon. Ropes are generally not required if you are comfortable on scrambling terrain. Both routes to the Castle Mountain Hut involve scrambling, as does the Fay Hut approach (for a very short section).

- ***Technical Rock Climbing***

This is full-on climbing with ropes and hardware. The Perren Route to the Neil Colgan Hut is typical of this terrain. Keep in mind that big boots and heavy packs may make the given grade harder than anticipated.

- ***Logging Road – 4x4 Recommended***

It is possible to drive almost any road described in this book in a vehicle with high clearance, or even an old car that you don't care much about. Keep in mind, however, that road conditions can deteriorate while you are at the hut, and a vehicle which got you way back on the logging roads in good conditions may not get you out again in bad conditions. The roads in the Selkirks to the Fairy Meadow and Great Cairn Huts are examples of this kind of terrain.

• ***Full-on Bushwhacking***

No trail. None. No fun either. The worst bushwhacking is found on the Goat Glacier and the Palmer Creek accesses to the Great Cairn Hut.

• ***Mountain Biking***

There are some trails (mostly in Jasper) where it is advantageous to bike part way. A bike is not essential, but it is an option which may save you some time. Fryatt and Mt. Colin Huts are examples.

• ***River Crossing (in boats)***

Likewise, there are some trails (again, in Jasper) where you could save some time with a boat.

• ***River Crossing (no boat)***

Some access routes involve crossing fairly major streams and creeks. When you see this icon you can expect that you will be getting your feet wet. The Perren Route to the Colgan Hut, the approach to the Lloyd MacKay Hut and the routes to the Great Cairn Hut all involve getting your feet wet.

• ***Glacier Travel***

Glacier travel is the most dangerous mode of travel to the huts and where you see this icon it is a mandatory part of the experience. Do not take these routes lightly. You must be equipped for crevasse rescue and all the members of your party must be experienced in the necessary skills. Two or more people are mandatory for these routes. Examples of this type of travel are the "Death Trap" route to Abbot, all routes to Neil Colgan and crossing the Wapta Icefields.

• ***Bear Warning***

This icon denotes access routes which involve travel in serious bear country where bear activity is not monitored by National Parks.

• ***Helicopter Accessible***

Huts which are located in National Parks are not accessible by helicopter. However, the Grassi, Great Cairn and Fairy Meadow Huts are not in National Parks and are regularly accessed this way.

• ***Track Skiing***

Some huts are accessed by a straightforward ski in the winter; the fireroad to the Elizabeth Parker Hut at Lake O'Hara is an example.

• ***Backcountry Skiing***

Winter access to some huts involves harder skiing, more serious terrain and more challenging route-finding. The Stanley Mitchell and the Wapta Huts come to mind.

• ***Hut to Hut Travel***

This denotes huts from which you can travel to another ACC hut within one day of travel. The Wapta huts would be in this category, as would the Fairy Meadow to Great Cairn trip at the more serious end of the scale.

• ***Objective Danger***

This icon denotes access routes which have objective danger from falling rocks, seracs or various other natural debris. While most mountain routes have some form of objective danger, the "Death Trap" and Fuhrmann Ledges routes to Abbot and the Schlesser Ledges to the Colgan Hut are worth mentioning particularly.

• *Avalanche Hazard*

Some approach routes may be threatened by avalanches, and routes denoted by this icon are certainly at danger in some seasons. Avalanche hazard may also be present on routes which are not designated with this icon. Check with Park Wardens, or phone the Canadian Avalanche Association for current conditions before setting out.

FACILITIES

This section of the hut description will give you all the information you need about the facilities you will find at the hut, where things are located and how they work. Included is information on the hut, its capacity, source of heat, specific equipment supplied for cooking and eating, and location of the outhouses. Some things which you should keep in mind at all the huts are:

Water

All water below treeline can carry viruses, such as *giardia,* and should be boiled or filtered before it is consumed. Water in the alpine is much safer and can usually be drunk untreated.

Garbage

With the exception of what can be burned (assuming there is a wood stove), everything that you take with you to the hut and do not consume must be carried out. Keep this in mind when you are planning your meals.

OPPORTUNITIES

This section gives an overview of the type and quality of recreational activities found in the area, along with applicable guide book references. Some specific routes, tours, and climbs are mentioned in greater detail where there is insufficient guide book information.

• *Trail Hiking*

This denotes extensive hiking on National Park trails in the immediate area. The fabulous day hiking trails around Lake O'Hara and the Elizabeth Parker Hut come immediately to mind.

• ***Scrambling***

The same as the access icon, but done as recreation. The Elizabeth Parker and Stanley Mitchell Huts, as well as the front country facilities provide access to this type of terrain.

• ***Mountaineering***

This could be technical or non-technical climbing; it generally requires a rope, and often involves glacier travel. It could include rock climbing, but of a mountainous and less technical nature, such as the Lougheed Traverse which is accessed from the Clubhouse, or Mt. Bowlen from the Neil Colgan Hut.

• ***Alpine Rock Climbing***

This is referred to as "alpine" to differentiate it from cragging and sport climbing. It generally does not include any snow or ice climbing (this would make it mountaineering), but it could have a glacier approach, such as in the Adamants and Gothic ranges around the Fairy Meadow and Great Cairn Huts.

• ***Sport Climbing***

Sport climbing refers to bolted climbs accessed from the hut directly. Only one hut (Castle Mountain) and the two front country facilities give access to this type of climbing.

• ***Track Skiing***

You'll see this icon where there are good track-set trails to ski on from the hut. The two front country facilities offer excellent track skiing.

• ***Ski Touring***

This icon means that there is good telemarking or alpine skiing terrain within close reach of the hut. The Fairy Meadow and the A.O. Wheeler Huts are the best examples of this.

• ***Ski Mountaineering***

This refers to climbing a mountain primarily on skis. The huts on the Wapta provide this type of terrain.

• ***Ice Climbing***

This icon is included only if it is normal to base yourself at the hut for the waterfall routes in question. The Elizabeth Parker Hut puts you in great shape to climb *Sad and Beautiful World*, for example.

• ***Resort Skiing***

This is a front country thing. The CAC is ten minutes from Skiing Louise, and the Canmore Clubhouse gives guests access to four or more hills in the area.

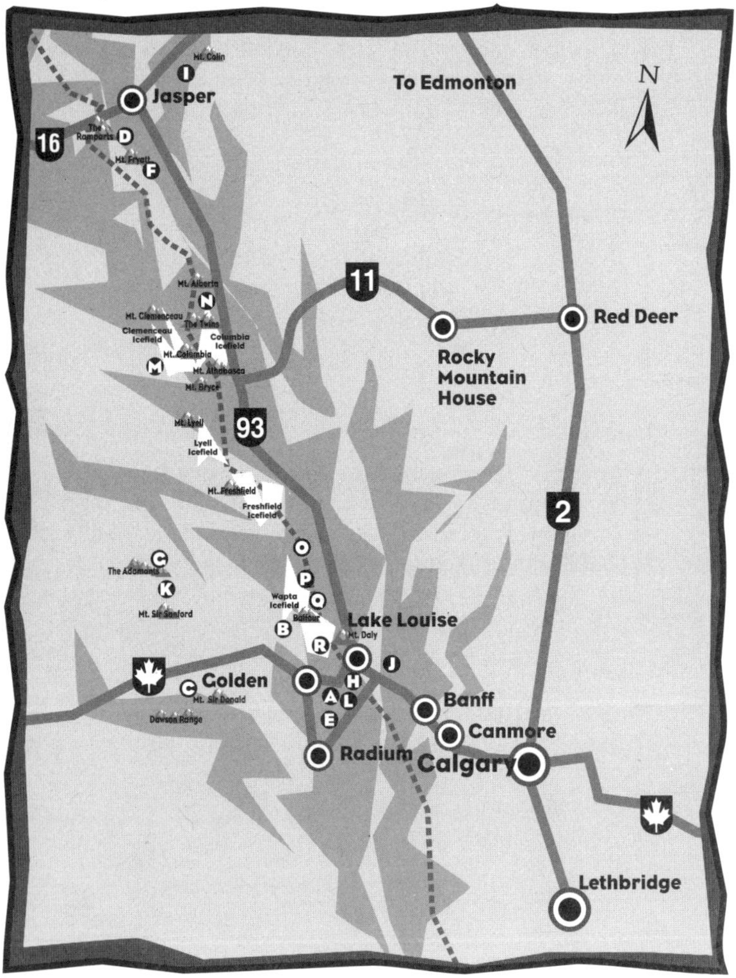

ACC Huts

A Elizabeth Parker
B Stanley Mitchell
C A.O. Wheeler
D Wates-Gibson
E Fay
F Sydney Vallance (Fryatt)
G Fairy Meadow
H Abbot Pass
I Mt. Colin Centennial
J Castle Mountain
K Great Cairn
L Neil Colgan
M Lawrence Grassi
N Lloyd MacKay (Mt. Alberta)
O Peter & Catharine Whyte (Peyto)
P Bow
Q Balfour
R Scott Duncan

Front Country Facilities

The Canmore Clubhouse and the Canadian Alpine Centre and International Hostel at Lake Louise are the two ACC "Front Country" facilities. The Clubhouse and Alpine Centre are both modern facilities with showers and full kitchens, and are drive-up accessible. These two facilities make excellent jumping off points for backcountry trips and bases for drying gear out after trips. The Alpine Centre is managed by the Southern Alberta Hostelling Association (SAHA), and takes its own reservations. The Canmore Clubhouse is also home to the Club's national office, making it convenient to pick up information, guide books and maps during your stay.

The Canmore Clubhouse

LOCATION

General Location

The Clubhouse is located 4.5 km northeast of the town of Canmore, on a bench above the highway on the sunny north side of the Bow Valley. It is close to the amenities of Canmore and Banff, yet maintains a quiet and relaxed atmosphere.

Map References

Canmore is found 110 km west of Calgary and 20 km east of Banff on any road map. The grid reference is 185596 on topographical map 82O/3 (Canmore).

Altitude

The approximate altitude of the Clubhouse is 4,380 ft. (1,335 m).

Hours of Operation

The Clubhouse hours are 9:00 am to 9:00 pm, seven days per week. The office is closed from 1:00 pm to 5:00 pm on Saturdays and Sundays during April, May, October and November

Rates and Reservations

All bunks at the Clubhouse are charged on a per person/per night basis. For Clubhouse rates, see the rates sheet insert (p. 18). Reservations for the Clubhouse are made through the national office. Phone (403) 678-3200, fax (403) 678-3224 or Email alpclub@telusplanet.net. ACC memberships are available at the Clubhouse and can be purchased on arrival, or by phone in advance.

ACCESS

You do not need a vehicle to get to the Clubhouse, but it does help. The Clubhouse is located a fair ways outside of the town of Canmore, and is not serviced by public transportation, except taxis. The Trans-Canada (#1) Highway provides easy access to the town of Canmore from both the east and west. There are signs at the turn-offs from the highway which direct you to the Clubhouse.

From Calgary via #1 Highway

Follow the Trans-Canada west to the first turn-off for the town of Canmore. The exit from the #1 brings you immediately to a "T" intersection at the 1A Highway. To the right (west) is the town of Canmore, to the left (east) is Exshaw. Proceed toward Exshaw for 1.5 km until it is possible to turn left onto Indian Flats Road. The Clubhouse is located at the end of Indian Flats Road, approximately 1 km from the 1A highway.

From Banff via #1 Highway

Driving from the west, there are three exits for the town of Canmore, the third of which provides the best access to the Clubhouse. This exit is signed "East 1A Highway – Exshaw." At the intersection of the 1A Highway, turn left toward Exshaw and continue to the Clubhouse as for the directions above.

Without a Vehicle

It is possible to walk to the Clubhouse from downtown Canmore, but the trip will take about 45 minutes. Walking takes the same route as driving from Canmore, following the 1A Highway to the east. Canmore is serviced by two taxi companies: Kananaskis Taxi (678-7667) and Canmore Taxi and Tours (678-0888). Both companies operate 24 hours a day, and the rates from downtown to the Clubhouse are around $8.

FACILITIES

The main Clubhouse building, the Bell Cabin and the PanAbode are collectively referred to as the Clubhouse. The buildings have some different facilities, but for the most part are very similar. All beds are bunk and dormitory style in rooms which accommodate either four or six people. Whenever possible, we will attempt to accommodate your group in the same room; however, we do not reserve specific bunks and all rooms are co-ed.

You will need to bring a sleeping bag (although we do have blankets and sheets for rent if you forget), toiletries and a pair of slippers or other indoor footwear. We do not have a cafe or food service of any kind, so you will have to bring all of your own groceries from town.

The Clubhouse Building

With the exception of groceries, the Clubhouse is equipped to provide you with everything you will need during your stay, be it as a one night jumping off point to the backcountry or for longer term recreating in the Canmore area. The main building sleeps 28 people in six separate rooms upstairs. There are washrooms down the hall from the accommodation rooms, and washrooms and showers in the basement. The main floor has a very cozy living room with a library of mountain literature and a fireplace — perfect for putting your feet up in front of after relaxing in the downstairs sauna. The Clubhouse is licensed, and beer and snacks are available from the reception desk.

There are storage lockers and coin-operated laundry machines which come in handy for guests on longer stays. To keep you in touch with the rest of the world there is a pay phone in the lobby and the office staff will send or receive faxes for you for a small fee.

To help you with your trip planning, or to complete your library at home, there is an excellent selection of local guide books and maps. In the Guides' Room downstairs, audio-visual equipment is available to large groups for lessons and lectures, or to individuals perusing their ice climbing slides.

The Bell Cabin

The Bell Cabin is a private, self-contained accommodation facility which is perfect for large groups (up to 15 people) or a couple of families. The building has a completely equipped kitchen, two washrooms and showers, a large, bright living room with a fireplace, and a beautiful view over the Bow Valley from the deck.

The Bell Cabin can be booked for single nights, or for longer stays. The price per night, as with all ACC facilities, will depend on the number of members and non-members in the group. Minimum group size to reserve the Bell Cabin is 10 people.

The PanAbode

The PanAbode sleeps four people very comfortably in a small building remote from the main Clubhouse and Bell Cabin. The PanAbode is equipped with a kitchen, living room and full bathroom, and has terrific views from its large deck.

The PanAbode can be booked for periods of one week or longer. Call the national office for pricing details.

OPPORTUNITIES

Canmore, summer and winter, is recreation central. From ice climbing to resort skiing to big wall alpine rock climbing, there are very few mountain recreation opportunities that cannot be done in the Canmore area. For some activities, Canmore has the very best.

Mountaineering

Mt. Joffre and Mt. Sir Douglas in the Kananaskis, and Mt. Stanley down the Radium Highway to the west, are big mountains with very good snow and ice routes. For rock ridges, faces and mountain traverses, the selection is enormous. The Kananaskis and the front ranges have excellent routes both close to the road and remote, mostly in the grade II and III range. Complete information on these types of routes can be obtained by referring to ***Selected Alpine Climbs in the Canadian Rockies*** and ***The Rocky Mountains of Canada – South.***

Alpine Rock Climbing

The Canmore area has the highest concentration of alpine rock climbing routes on big walls in the Rockies. The climbing varies from sunny 5.5 routes on the west end of Mt. Yamnuska, to a grade VI 5.11 A4 route on the Windtower, to multi pitch bolted sport climbs on Chinaman's Peak and the east end of Rundle. Up and down the Bow Valley, from the foothills to Castle Mountain, the area accessible from Canmore and the Clubhouse provides many decades worth of projects on long limestone walls. The most popular cliffs include Mt. Yamnuska, the east end of Rundle (EEOR), Chinaman's Peak, Mt. Louis, the Wild West Wall in the Ghost River, the CMC Valley and Castle Mountain. Information on these routes can be found in ***Bow Valley Rock, Kananaskis Rock, Sport Climbs in the Canadian Rockies*** and ***Selected Alpine Climbs in the Canadian Rockies.***

Sport Climbing

Equally as extensive as the multi-pitch alpine rock climbing is the area's single pitch cragging. Primarily in the limestone canyons accessed from the major highways, the climbs include 5.3 routes on pure friction slabs at Wasootch, 5.13+ projects on the stunning overhanging pocketed walls at Acephale, and everything in between. There are more than 20 different climbing areas within an hour or less drive of the Clubhouse giving access to more than 1,000 sport climbs. The most popular areas are Cougar and Grotto canyons (the former is accessible on foot from the Clubhouse) and "The Back of the Lake" crags at Lake Louise. Complete topo-format information on these routes can be found in ***Sport Climbs in the Canadian Rockies*** and ***Kananaskis Rock.***

Scrambling

The book ***Scrambles in the Canadian Rockies*** lists 55 scrambling routes on peaks in Kananaskis Country and the Bow Valley before you even get to Lake Louise. Lady MacDonald and Grotto Mountain can be climbed starting from the Clubhouse parking lot, and dozens more are within 15 minutes drive.

Day Hiking

The day hikes in the area are only limited by your imagination. There are dozens of hikes on established and maintained trails in the immediate area recorded in ***The Canadian Rockies Trail Guide, Banff-Assiniboine: A Beautiful World*** and ***Kananaskis Country Trail Guide.*** Cory Pass in Banff National Park and Wind Pass overlooking Canmore and the Wind Valley are not far from the Clubhouse and provide amazing views. Heart Creek, Carrot Creek and Grotto Canyon are beautiful hikes without much elevation gain (the latter having the added attraction of ancient Native pictographs visible from the trail) and are also very close to home. The Bourgeau Lake and Chester Lake trails are two examples of hikes which take you to impressive mountain lakes within a couple hours of leaving your vehicle. I can barely begin to describe the trails; get a guidebook and make some plans.

Backcountry Skiing

The best ski touring and ski mountaineering accessible from the Clubhouse is in Kananasksis Country, which has a little bit of everything. Mt. Black Prince is an excellent telemark slope, Mt. Joffre is the classic ski mountaineering peak of the area, and the French/Haig/Robertson Glacier circuit provides a great glacier traverse outing. These outings are described in detail in ***Summits and Icefields*** and ***Kananaskis Country Ski Trails.***

Track Skiing

Cross country ski trails are one of the things that Kananaskis Country is famous for. The guidebook to the area, ***Kananaskis Country Ski Trails*** covers a huge number of groomed trails, backcountry trails and mountain routes, all of which are accessible from the Clubhouse in less than an hour. Chic Scott's ***Ski Trails in the Canadian Rockies*** covers some of the same terrain as the Kananaskis guide, but in lesser detail, and then covers the best of the trails into the Banff area, and beyond. One of the attractions of the Kananaskis area is the fabulous track set areas with groomed trails. This includes the Kananaskis Lakes area, Mt. Shark and the Canmore Nordic Centre, the site of the nordic events of the 1988 Winter Olympics. These areas are well maintained and groomed. The Canmore Nordic Centre charges a nominal day-use fee, while Mount Shark and Kananaskis Lakes areas are free of charge.

Resort Skiing

Five downhill ski resorts are located within a one hour drive of the Canmore Clubhouse. There are two resorts, Nakiska and Fortress Mountain, in Kananaskis Country to the south; Sunshine and Mt. Norquay are very close to the town of Banff; and Skiing Louise is a little further down the road at Lake Louise.

Ice Climbing

The Clubhouse has long been a centre for ice climbing and a meeting place for ice climbers in the Bow Valley. Between the Kananaskis, Ghost River, Canmore and Banff areas (the areas readily accessible from Canmore) there are more than 150 ice climbs to choose from. The climbs range from roadside grade 2s to grade 7+s high on Mt. Rundle. This area has enough climbing to keep the dedicated waterfall climber busy for several seasons. Joe Josephson, in the third edition of ***Waterfall Ice,*** details the routes, approaches and local history; if you are waterfall climbing in the Canmore area, you definitely need this book.

The Canadian Alpine Centre and International Hostel at Lake Louise

LOCATION

General Location

The CAC is located on Pipestone Rd. in the Village of Lake Louise in Banff National Park. Lake Louise is on the Trans-Canada Highway, three hours west of Calgary, and a five-hour drive from Edmonton.

Map References

The Village of Lake Louise is found on any road map of Alberta, very close to the junction of the Trans-Canada (#1) Highway and Highway 93. The topographical map of the area is 82N/8, and the CAC is located at grid reference 568974.

Altitude

The CAC is at approximately 5,050 ft. (1,540m).

Hours of Operation

The reception desk is open from 8:00 am to 10:00 pm on weekdays, and from 7:00 am to 10:00 pm on weekends. There is also 24-hour access and check-in with the night person.

Rates and Reservations

For current rates, call the Canadian Alpine Centre at (403) 522-2200. Memberships in both Hostelling International and The Alpine Club of Canada are honoured.

The CAC offers dormitory rooms and two-bed rooms at different rates. The dorm rooms sleep either four or six people, have a washroom in the room and a shower down the hall

Reservations for the CAC require a deposit in advance equal to the first night's fee. For groups of 10 or more and for private rooms, reservations are mandatory all year. Reservations are also strongly recommended for June through September, and Christmas, spring break and weekends during ski season. Visa and Mastercard are accepted. Reservations may be made by telephone, fax or mail.

The Canadian Alpine Centre & International Hostel at Lake Louise can be reached at (403)522-2200 (phone), 522-2253 (fax) or by mail at Box 115, Lake Louise, Alberta, Canada, T0L 1E0.

ACCESS

From the #1 Highway

There is only one exit from the Trans-Canada (#1) Highway to the townsite of Lake Louise, which takes you to a four-way stop on Village Road. Turn right at the stop sign and follow Village Road west for slightly less than a kilometre to a turn off and a sign for the CAC on the left side of the road.

Without a Vehicle

Lake Louise is serviced by Greyhound Bus Lines several times a day from both the east and the west on the #1 Highway. The bus arrives in Lake Louise at Samson Mall in the centre of the village. From the mall, the CAC is a five-minute walk along the river or down Village Road.

FACILITIES

The Building and Accommodation

Guests of the CAC are provided with a choice of accommodation options, including one-, two-, four-, and six-bed rooms, ensuite bathrooms and private showers; overall there are beds for up to 150 guests in two separate buildings. There are meeting rooms for larger groups, laundry facilities, bright spacious lounges with fireplaces, a library, games room, sauna and a workshop for ski and bike repairs. The CAC also provides completely equipped self-catering kitchens for groups wishing to prepare their own meals, and the excellent Bill Peyto's Cafe for those who wish to have others prepare their meals. Bill Peyto's is a licensed cafe offering huge, tasty breakfasts, lunches and dinners. They also have cappucinos, baked goods, and a beautiful patio.

OPPORTUNITIES

The Canadian Alpine Centre provides year-round access to backcountry recreational opportunities in the Lake Louise area. If you come to the mountains to recreate, chances are you can do it in the Lake Louise area.

Mountaineering

The Lake Louise group of the Rocky Mountains has excellent mountaineering at all levels. The east slopes of Mt. Aberdeen provide a moderate outing on a glacier with outstanding views from the summit. The East Ridge of Unnamed Peak is one of the area's forgotten gems of moderate rock climbing and the Greenwood/Locke Route on Mt. Temple is one of the all-time classic north face routes of the Canadian Rockies. These and dozens of other routes are accessible from the CAC in day outings. ***Selected Alpine Climbs in the Canadian Rockies*** and ***The Rocky Mountains of Canada – South*** have complete details of the mountaineering routes around Lake Louise.

Alpine Rock Climbing

The cliffs on Castle Mountain 30 km to the east provide some of the best alpine rock climbing in the area. Climbs on Castle Mountain can be made much more conveniently from a base in the Castle Mountain Hut (refer to hut description), but are also regularly done from the road in a day. Another excellent outing in the Lake Louise area is the Grand Sentinel. This amazing quartzite spire is almost 300 ft. high, and has several routes to 5.9 which are well worth the long walk. Other alpine rock outings in the area include the East Face of Mt. Babel, IV, 5.11, and the less serious routes on the Tower of Babel. The best source of information for these routes is ***Selected Alpine Climbs in the Canadian Rockies,*** and to a lesser extent ***The Rocky Mountains of Canada – South.***

Sport Climbing

The very best single pitch climbing in the entire Rocky Mountains is at Lake Louise. The very, very fine quartzite cliffs at "The Back of the Lake" have something for everyone, with grades from 5.2 to 5.12d. The beautiful purple and orange quartzite rock is not common in the Rockies, and provides excellent climbing on both bolted and naturally protected climbs. A number of climbers who have travelled extensively in Europe and the U.S. have commented that the climbing is as good, and the area as beautiful, as anywhere they have been. Quite a compliment! If the cragging at Lake Louise has a down side, it is the season. It is very rare that the area is too hot, and toques and mitts while belaying are often *de rigueur* on cold days in July and August. On hot summer days, though, there is nowhere finer in the world to be cragging. ***Sport Climbs of the Canadian Rockies*** has all the beta.

Scrambling

The vast glaciation of the peaks in the Lake Louise group does not lend itself to scrambling as much as it does to mountaineering, but there are truly some gems. Mt. Temple, the highest peak in the Lake Louise group, and one of the highest summits in the Canadian Rockies, is perhaps the best known and most sought after scrambling peak in the area. Mt. Fairview, on the other hand, living up to its name, provides one of the most spectacular views of any scrambling peak anywhere. There are almost 40 peaks which provide scrambling opportunities in the Lake Louise area;. The book ***Scrambles in the Canadian Rockies*** details these routes.

Day Hiking

Outstanding floral meadows, alpine lakes, mountain sheep, towering mountain walls, golden larches, panoramas from passes and ridges — Lake Louise has it all. To hike all of the existing trails in the area would take years; to hike them all in the different seasons and conditions, to see everything there is to see would take a lifetime. The trails are as casual as a stroll around Lake Louise or as involved as multi-day backpacking adventures. ***The Canadian Rockies Trail Guide*** by Patton and Robinson, ***Hiking Lake Louise*** by Mike Potter and ***The World of Lake Louise*** by Don Beers are the best of the guide books to the hikes in the area.

Backcountry Skiing

Chic Scott's ***Summits and Icefields*** lists telemark slopes close to the road, peaks in the area for ski mountaineering, and classic icefield outings and traverses. There is plenty to do in the immediate area of Lake Louise, but that does not stop skiers from driving up to the Columbia Icefields for day trips to check out the snow there too.

The Wapta Icefield is a very short distance up Highway 93 north, but is more commonly used for overnight outings based out of the Bow or other ACC huts on the icefields.

Track Skiing

From shuffling across the frozen Lake Louise itself, to skiing in and out from Skoki in a day, the Lake Louise area has track skiing for everyone. Once again, Chic Scott's ***Ski Trails in the Canadian Rockies*** is the book to have - it lists almost 50 trails around Lake Louise and Skoki, down the #1 into Yoho Park and up the first part of the Icefields Parkway.

Resort Skiing

The Skiing Louise ski resort is right here. The hill is less than a ten-minute drive from the CAC, and through the ski season (especially on weekends) it is possible to pick up rides to the hill with other guests.

Ice Climbing

The entire Rocky Mountains is an ice climbing playground, and since the CAC is a front country facility (ie. you can see your car in the parking lot from your bunk), there is access to most of the waterfalls in the range in a day. If ice climbers from Calgary drive up to the Weeping Wall for a day of climbing (sometimes twice in a weekend), it should not be out of the question to access just about any road-side route in the range from Lake Louise. The most easily accessed climbs from the CAC include *Louise Falls* at the back of the lake, *Linda Ice Nine* slightly further along the trail to the teahouse, and the famous beer climbs at Field. Take Joe Josephson's book ***Waterfall Ice,*** sit down by the fire in the lounge, or over a little cappucino in Bill Peyto's Cafe, and let yourself dream.

Simon Parboosingh
on the* Liquid Sky Wall, *Lake Louise
A friend who passed away, 1994

He wakes or sleeps with the enduring dead;
thou canst not soar where he is sitting now –
Dust to the dust! but the pure spirit shall flow
Back to the burning fountain whence it came,
A portion of the Eternal.

Adonais, Percy Bysshe Shelley

The Lake Louise Area

ACC Huts

A Elizabeth Parker
B Stanley Mitchell
E Fay
H Abbot Pass
J Castle Mountain
L Neil Colgan

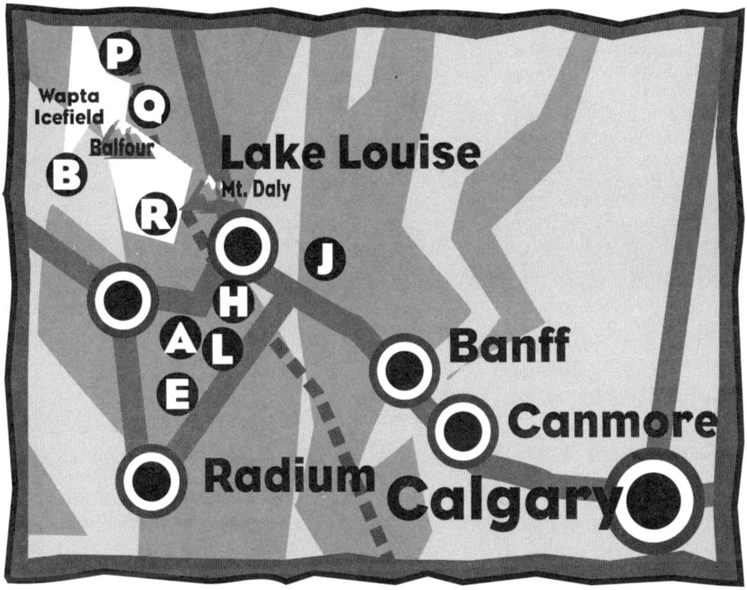

The Lake Louise area is home to the oldest and most well-known huts in the Rockies.

The four Class A huts in the area average nearly 70 years old. The Neil Colgan Hut is the highest permanent structure in Canada; the Abbot Pass Hut is second, and one of the most famous back-country shelters in North America. The huts are generally easy to access, and this, combined with their location in the famous Lake Louise area, makes them some of the most popular in the ACC system — in the summer they can be very busy. The Class B huts (Neil Colgan and Castle Mountain) are climbers' huts, with technical accesses.

The Elizabeth Parker Hut

HISTORY

Elizabeth Parker:

As much as any single person, Elizabeth Parker was responsible for the formation of the Alpine Club of Canada. For many years A. O. Wheeler had a desire to begin a Canadian alpine club "similar to the European and other big alpine clubs of the world representing mountain ranges such as the Canadian Cordillera," but could not rouse sufficient interest and support, meeting instead with skepticism and indifference. In 1902, in a conversation at Glacier House with Charles Fay, Wheeler decided to form a Canadian chapter of the American Alpine Club, which Fay was in the process of forming. When Wheeler tried to garner support for the idea through the country's leading newspapers, Elizabeth Parker, then on the staff of the Winnipeg Free Press, chastised him for his lack of patriotism. Wheeler asked Parker to support his plan "A," a truly Canadian club, and got it in spades. As Wheeler said of the Club's founder: "Her cultured and forcible style of writing, her keen sense of vision and invariable accuracy of statement was one of the most helpful factors of the Club's foundation." Largely due to the efforts of Elizabeth Parker and the Winnipeg Free Press, the Alpine Club of Canada was formed in Winnipeg on March 27, 1906; Mrs. Parker was one of six original honorary members.

The Elizabeth Parker Hut:

The present Wiwaxy cabin was the first hut in the Lake O'Hara area, built in 1912 by the Canadian Pacific Railway. This was the same year that the ACC applied for and was granted a two-acre lease for a future hut on the south shore of Lake O'Hara, the site of the Club's 1909 annual camp. In 1919, the CPR built the present Elizabeth Parker Hut, and by 1923 had built a further 11 huts in the meadow. In 1923/24, the CPR moved all but the first two huts down to the lakeshore, and seven years later donated the last two in the meadow to the ACC. The Club was able to exchange its lakeshore lease for a meadow lease, and in 1931 was in business with a hut at Lake O'Hara — the Elizabeth Parker Hut.

As you can expect with log buildings in alpine conditions constructed early in the century, the Elizabeth Parker Hut has required substantial renovations and upkeep. Over the years the hut has seen a new floor, a new roof, new timbers and new foundation logs, as well as completely new interior furnishings. The outhouses are new, a stove in the Wiwaxy Cabin has been added and the entire meadow around the hut has been rehabilitated and reseeded. Over the past couple of years, the Huts Committee has worked very hard to restore the appearance of the hut as closely as possible to its original state. The Canadian government recognized the Elizabeth Parker Hut as a federal historic building in 1987.

"...her memory is preserved by the very popular tribute inscribed with her name, the 'Elizabeth Parker Hut', maintained in one of the most charming centres of the Canadian Rockies, close by beautiful Lake O'Hara."

(Quotation from Elizabeth Parker's obituary
by A. O. Wheeler, *CAJ* #29.)

LOCATION

General Location

The hut is in Yoho National Park, in the alpine meadow approximately 0.5 km west of Lake O'Hara. The Elizabeth Parker Hut is not the "Alpine Club" cabin marked on the south shore of Lake O'Hara on map 82N/8.

Map Reference

The hut and the approach to the hut are on 82N/8, as are all of the hiking, skiing and climbing objectives in the area. This is the only map you will need.

Grid Reference

The hut is located at 457893.

Altitude

The hut sits at 6,700 ft. (2,040 m).

SUMMER ACCESS:

The most common way of approaching the hut is via the Lake O'Hara road and a trail to the west from its end. The road is serviced in the summer months (mid-June to the end of September) by a Parks Canada bus which picks passengers up at the Lake O'Hara parking lot four times daily. The road is not open to private vehicles at any time. The road can be hiked (although a much more scenic hike into the area is the Cataract Brook Trail), but mountain bikes are not permitted.

Parks Canada requests that larger parties of hikers do not travel together, but rather split up into smaller parties to reduce the impact on the experience of other hikers in the area.

Lake O'Hara via the Parks Canada Bus

This is the easiest and fastest way into the lake and the hut. With the recent implementation of bus reservations through the ACC office, it is far more convenient than in the past.

Net Elevation Gain

From the Lake O'Hara parking lot, the road rises 1,300 ft. to the lake.

Time

The bus ride takes 20 to 30 minutes from the parking lot to the second stop at the lake; the walk from where the bus stops is about another 15 minutes.

Approach

The bus, the hike up the road and the Cataract Brook Trail all begin at the Lake O'Hara parking lot 12 km west of Lake Louise village (13 km east of Field). The parking lot turnoff is well signed on the Trans Canada Highway. Follow the road across the railway tracks, take an immediate right turn onto a gravel road and follow it a short distance to the Lake O'Hara parking lot. At the parking lot you will find a Parks Canada information board which marks the meeting place for the bus and the trailhead for the hike up the road to the lake.

Bus Reservations

Bus reservations for guests staying at the Elizabeth Parker and Abbot Pass Huts are made at the same time as the hut booking. Each of the morning buses going in to Lake O'Hara has a reservation quota of 12 for ACC Hut passengers. These spaces are booked on a first-come-first-served basis at the ACC office. The afternoon buses do not have a quota for ACC passengers, and are typically less crowded. (The bus fees as of June 1997 are $12 per adult, $5 per child between 6-16; kids under 6 ride for free. Fares include the return trip from the lake; seats on outgoing buses do not need to be reserved).

Meeting The Bus

Buses depart the Lake O'Hara parking lot at 8:30 and 10:30 am, and 4:30 and 7:30 pm, Mountain (Alberta) Time. You should arrive 30 minutes in advance to confirm your reservation with the Parks staff and load your gear onto the bus. On the bus you will be given information about trail closures, bears and the facilities at Lake O'Hara. The bus ride takes approximately 20 minutes from the parking lot to the second stop at the lake where the hikes to the Elizabeth Parker and Abbot Pass huts begin (the first stop is for the campground).

From The Bus Stop

From the second stop at Lake O'Hara, follow the signed trail to the "Alpine Meadows." The trail begins immediately to the right of the Le Relais Day Use Shelter (just across the road from the wardens' cabin) and climbs up a small hill into the trees. On the other side of the treed hill, the trail descends a short distance and then turns right and follows Schäffer creek to the Alpine Meadows and the Elizabeth Parker Hut. This is a pretty casual hike, taking 15 minutes or less.

Day use

The ACC can take bus reservations only for hut guests. Day-users of the Lake O'Hara area must make their reservations through the Yoho Park Information Centre in Field. The information centre is open Monday to Saturday from 8:00 am to 4:30 pm, Mountain Time, and can be reached at (250) 343-6433.

The Cataract Brook Trail

This is an alternative to catching the bus into the Lake O'Hara area, or to hiking along the dusty fireroad that the bus drives. It adds a couple of kilometres to the approach, but the scenery, which includes avalanche paths, boulder fields, meadows and alpine lakes, more than makes up for the extra half hour or so.

Net elevation gain

From the Lake O'Hara parking lot to the hut you will gain approximately 1,450 ft.

Time

This approach will take you about three to four hours to hike from the parking lot to the hut.

Approach

Begin the hike on a trail which starts beside the pit toilets at the very southern end of the Lake O'Hara parking lot. The trail heads southwest through the forest, crosses Cataract Brook and heads more southerly. After another kilometre or so, the trail intersects the old fire road. Do not follow the fireroad; cross it and follow the trail as it continues on the other side. The trail gains elevation continually along the east slopes of Cathedral Mountain, passing Narao Lakes, a large boulder field and many avalanche slopes. The trail levels off and continues without much elevation gain for about a kilometre, crosses Duchesnay Creek and comes to a four-way trail intersection. To the right are Linda Lakes; to the left, Lake O'Hara via the Parks Canada Campground; and straight ahead are Morning Glory Lakes. The trail to the Elizabeth Parker Hut follows the trail to Morning Glory Lakes, passes them, contours around a forested buttress on the east side of Odaray Mountain and descends slightly into the Alpine Meadow.

WINTER ACCESS

Winter access is almost exclusively by skiing up the fireroad, and the route-finding is not difficult. It is not advisable to ski the Cataract Brook Trail in the winter due to the very high avalanche danger contouring across the east side of Cathedral Mountain (more than half of the distance of the trail to the hut).

Lake O'Hara Fireroad

Net Elevation Gain

The elevation gain is approximately 1,450 ft.

Time

Three to four hours is standard for this ski. Some parties can make the trip in under two and a half hours with light packs when the track is well set, but parties with improper gear or too much baggage have taken seven hours or more because they thought the hut was "just a little afternoon ski from the parking lot." This hut is definitely backcountry in the winter; do not underestimate it.

Approach

The parking lot and trailhead are the same in the winter as they are in the summer. Start skiing up the road, and follow it to the wardens' cabin at Lake O'Hara. On the opposite side of the road from the wardens' cabin is the Le Relais Day Shelter, and an outhouse. The route to the hut follows the trail which starts in between the two buildings and climbs steeply through the trees for a short distance. On the other side of the hill the trail turns right and follows the creek to the meadow and the Elizabeth Parker Hut.

FACILITIES

The Hut and Accommodation

The Elizabeth Parker Hut is actually two buildings: the main hut and the Wiwaxy Cabin. The main hut has a large kitchen area separated from the rest of the hut which holds the bunks, tables and wood-burning stove. The main building sleeps up to 16 people on two large, long bunks. The Wiwaxy Cabin does not have a kitchen area, but has a wood-burning stove and sleeps eight people comfortably. The capacity of the two huts is 24 people in the summer, and 20 in the winter. In the summer, part of the Wiwaxy Cabin is used by the custodian in residence, but not exclusively. It is not possible to reserve space in the Wiwaxy Cabin specifically; rather, all bunks in the two buildings are reserved generally — once you get to the hut, it is first come, first served.

Heat Source

There is a very good air-tight wood-burning stove in the common/accommodation area of the main hut, and, in the winter, a smaller wood-burning stove in the Wiwaxy Cabin. The wood supply is stored behind the Wiwaxy Cabin. Please replace all firewood you use in the hut with cut and split wood from the pile.

Cooking

The hut is supplied with all the dishes, pots and pans you will need, and is equipped with three two-burner propane stoves.

Propane:

The ACC supplies the propane for the stoves and the tanks are filled at the Lake O'Hara Lodge. We ask that you take all canisters which have been emptied by your group down to the lodge for refilling. They can be dropped off at the large wood pile on the west side of the lodge. If convenient, refilled canisters should be transported back to the hut. In the winter, the tanks will be refilled by ACC personnel.

Lighting

Lighting is provided by propane lanterns in the main building and by Coleman white gas lanterns in the Wiwaxy cabin.

Tools

There are water buckets, axes, saws, shovels and various tools. The axes and saws are located either inside the front door of the hut, or hung up by the wood pile.

Water Supply

The creek from Odaray Mountain which runs past the hut 30m to the north supplies the drinking water in the summer. There is a pipe which is easily accessible under the bridge. In the winter months may be possible to find some unfrozen pools under the snow at the junction of the two creeks approximately 80m northeast of the hut.

Grey Water

Grey water disposal is in a ground sump 15m southwest of the front door of the main hut, on the right side of the path to the outhouses. In the winter it may be necessary to excavate the sump.

Outhouses

The outhouses are 10m beyond the ground sump, 25m southwest of the front door of the main hut. Please do not dispose of any unnecessary garbage in the outhouses.

Garbage

Burn all paper garbage and food scraps, and pack out all other garbage and unused food. In the summer recycling is done by the Lake O'Hara Lodge, and all recyclables which are clean and separated may be taken to the Le Relais Day Shelter. Garbage can be deposited in Parks Canada containers at the campground. In the winter all garbage must be packed out.

OPPORTUNITIES

Mountaineering and Scrambling

The Lake O'Hara area is a high quality mountaineering area with a number of excellent climbs in extraordinarily beautiful surroundings. Most of the routes are on rock ridges, but there is the odd snow couloir (such as the routes on Ringrose and Glacier Peak) and glacier outing (such as the normal route on Odaray). The routes are generally of up to intermediate difficulty, with few "difficult" routes. The routes on Mts. Victoria and Lefroy from Abbot Pass are also accessible from Lake O'Hara in a day, although this is less common than climbing them from the pass. Information on these routes can be found in ***Selected Alpine Climbs in the Canadian Rockies, The Rocky Mountains of Canada – South*** and ***Scrambles in the Canadian Rockies.***

Ice Climbing

The scope of the ice climbing in the area is presently limited (only one route exists in the new guide book), but the potential for new routes is great. The hut could become a popular ice climbing destination with some dedicated development. There is potential for difficult new routes on Odaray Mountain and Mt. Huber as well as on the Mt. Victoria massif. The one established route is a classic Grade 4 on Wiwaxy Peak, and is best approached from the hut. Information on the climb can be found in ***Waterfall Ice Climbs in the Canadian Rockies.***

Day Hiking

More than any other activity, the Lake O'Hara area is renowned for the quantity and quality of day hiking. The hikes in the area vary from strolls around lakes and through meadows to more challenging hikes to passes. In addition to the trails, there are also several alpine routes from the lake. These routes are more serious, follow steeper and more exposed trails and gain more elevation than the hiking trails. All together, the well developed and maintained trail system gives access to six alpine valleys and 16 mountain lakes. Excellent information on the system of trails in the Lake O'Hara area can be found in ***The Canadian Rockies Trail Guide*** and ***The Wonder of Yoho.***

Backcountry Skiing

Skiing from the hut, like the hiking, is extensive. Many of the trails and alpine routes that are hiked in the summer are popular with backcountry skiers in the winter, and several slopes near the hut offer good telemarking terrain. The area is not covered in a ski touring guidebook, but summer trail books and a healthy concern for winter hazards will allow you to explore most of the area, and probably find some good slopes.

The Abbot Pass Hut

HISTORY

Abbot Pass is rich in the history of the development of the west and inextricably linked to the history of climbing and guiding in the Canadian Rockies. It was here that Phillip Stanley Abbot fell to his death while attempting the first ascent of Mt. Lefroy in 1896, giving North America its first mountaineering fatality and the pass its name. In 1897 Peter Sarbach, the first Swiss guide in Canada, led a group up Mt. Lefroy and Mt. Victoria and demonstrated the need for trained guides in Canada. The Canadian Pacific Railroad saw the potential for developing tourism in Canada and hired Swiss guides to work at their hotels. By the beginning of the 1920s, ascents of Victoria and Lefroy had become popular guided outings.

The CPR Cabin, as it was originally known, was built to provide easier access to the peaks, and to provide shelter in emergency situations. The construction, which was carried out by the Swiss guides working for the CPR, took place during the summer of 1922 and the hut was finished and officially opened in 1923.

By the 1960s the hut had been well used by both the CPR guides and the general public alike, and as it essentially had no upkeep or maintenance for 40 years, had become dilapidated and grimy. The CPR turned the hut over to Parks Canada, which, along with a dedicated group of volunteers, cleaned, gutted and re-roofed the place. In 1985, Parks turned the operation of the hut over to the ACC. The Club has since renovated the hut three times, once in 1986, again in 1993, and June of 1997 saw the interior of the hut brought back to close to its original state. The Abbot Pass Hut was designated a National Historic Site on August 26, 1997.

Today the Abbot Pass Hut is well used. Hikers use it as a destination for day hikes and overnight visits, while mountaineers base themselves in the hut for attempts on the classic climbs of

Victoria and Lefroy. The hut is as popular as ever with professional guides. However, the relative ease of access, spectacular setting and publicity have occasionally conspired to lure both hikers and climbers beyond their level of comfort. As traffic at the hut has increased, so has the concern for safety. Remaining true to the original goal of safety for mountaineers at the pass, an emergency telephone, the first at an Alpine Club of Canada hut, was installed in the fall of 1994. The Alpine Club national office and the Banff Park Wardens in Lake Louise can be contacted directly from the hut in the event of an accident or other emergency.

LOCATION

General Location

Abbot Pass is located between Mts. Victoria and Lefroy. Most people who have visited the Rockies, and many who have not, recognize Mt. Victoria as the backdrop to the postcard photos of Lake Louise, but perhaps do not know it by name. Abbot Pass is at the left end of the famous east ridge of Mt. Victoria, out of sight from the lake. The Continental Divide, the Banff National Park/ Yoho National Park border and the provincial boundary between Alberta and B.C. all run over the summits of Victoria and Lefroy and right through the pass. The hut is in the middle of the pass.

The view south from Abbot Pass

Map Reference

Map 82N/8 (Lake Louise) has everything you need for the approaches to the hut and the climbs.

Grid Reference

The hut is located at 495903 on 82N/8 (Lake Louise).

Altitude

The hut sits at 9,598 ft. (2,926m).

ACCESS

Few huts are as satisfying to reach as the Abbot Pass Hut. It is a majestic building that you can't see until you're almost standing in the doorway, and the pass has a truly alpine feel to it, even on the warmest summer days. It is the second highest (only the Neil Colgan Hut is higher) permanent, habitable structure in Canada. You know you have earned your dinner when you get there.

Lake O'Hara Access

This is by far the most popular route to the hut, despite the heinous scree slope at the end of the hike. It is safer, faster and less technical than the approach via the "Death Trap" or Fuhrmann Ledges Routes, and it travels through exceptionally beautiful hiking terrain. This route is the recommended approach to Abbot Pass.

Net Elevation Gain

From Lake O'Hara to the pass, the trail gains 3,000 ft.

Time

Standard time on this approach is four hours. On the fast side, three-hour times are not out of the question, but many parties take five hours or more. Approach times depend on how much time is taken on the scree slope. This trip is commonly underestimated by hikers and climbers alike, and a number of parties have unexpectedly spent a night out, either at the hut when they expected to come down the same day, or (worse) in the middle of the scree slope!

Approach

The first order of business is getting to Lake O'Hara. Refer to the approach description to the Elizabeth Parker Hut to get to the lake.

From Lake O'Hara, follow the signed trail to Lake Oesa. From the north side of Lake Oesa (the left side as you are approaching it), the trail continues up a talus slope and into a wide scree gully. You will find a Parks Canada sign signifying the end of the maintained trail, and the beginning of the alpine route to Abbot Pass. From the end of the marked trail the route ascends the gully for a ways, then breaks out to the right over quartzite ledges. Scramble up and right over these ledges then traverse out and right on a trail just below the cliffs to reach the bottom of the main scree slope. From here you are on your own for trails; pick whatever line looks best and begin pedalling uphill. There are usually cairns marking the general route, especially through the quartzite ledges. This scree slope is long and arduous, with about 1,500 vertical feet of elevation gain on loose shale and marbles. Do not underestimate it, and don't plan to get from Lake Oesa to the top in 15 minutes when you see the weather moving in.

"Death Trap" Access

At the turn of the century this was the logical route to the pass. Lake Louise was the alpine centre of the Canadian Rockies, there was no road to Lake O'Hara, no Parks Canada trail to Lake Oesa, and the glacier leading to the pass was considerably more mellow. The danger from falling seracs and the like from the upper Victoria Glacier has always been high. In recent years the glacier has become more crevasse riddled (particularly near the pass) and a large bergschrund running across the entire route has made it nearly impassable. This route is not the first choice for access to Abbot Pass, and is only for the strong alpinist. Check with the Banff Park Wardens at the Lake Louise Visitors' Centre for current conditions.

Note: This is a very serious alpine route which requires glacier travel and crevasse rescue skills. It should only be undertaken by experienced mountaineers and in the best conditions. Crevasses on the glacier and falling ice and seracs from the upper Victoria Glacier overhead pose serious danger.

Net Elevation Gain

From Lake Louise to the pass is a gain of about 3,900 ft.

Time

Times for this approach vary widely, and depend largely upon the amount of fresh snow, time required to deal with the crevasses, and difficulties encountered through the bergschrund itself. Certainly allow a full day, and get an early start to avoid the worst of the garbage falling off the upper Victoria Glacier.

Approach

From Lake Louise follow the trail to the Plain of Six Glaciers Tea House and the lookout beyond. If the weather is fair you will be able to see the pass and the hut. From here the route description is quite simple — descend to the Victoria Glacier and follow it up to the pass — but the complicated crevasses and objective hazards make it more serious. On the glacier, follow a line up the middle, or slightly to the Mt. Lefroy side, to avoid the danger of falling seracs from the upper Victoria Glacier. As the glacier steepens, there will be a large bergschrund to negotiate which may require technical ice climbing skills to cross or skirt it on the right side. It is a good idea to have a pair of short ice tools. In some years this bergschrund is simply not passable and parties should be prepared to turn around at this point. As the glacier approaches the pass it is heavily crevassed, and the best route through is to head left toward the Mt. Lefroy side of the glacier and contour back to the pass and the hut higher up. Use your own judgement here, as the glacier will undoubtedly change significantly in different seasons and years. Use great caution if using this route as a descent from the pass; the slope leading down toward the most heavily crevassed portion of the glacier is quite steep, making it difficult to arrest a fall into a crevasse.

"Fuhrmann Ledges" Access/Descent

As an alternative to the dangers of the "Death Trap," this route provides a safer, albeit more circuitous route to the pass or (more commonly) back to the lake. It incorporates portions of what was known as "the Old Swiss Guides Route"; however, the terrain has changed substantially since the beginning of the century. The first recorded use of this route in modern times was by Peter Fuhrmann, while guiding an Alpine Club "Rockies Panorama" hiking camp down from the pass in 1991 — a trip on which the participants surely got their money's worth! A trip up this route in the early season would have the advantage of snow covering the scree cone on the east face of Lefroy, possibly providing more secure footing. However, the upper west slopes of Lefroy get the afternoon sun and in the early season there is a greater possibility of debris falling from above as you traverse the final trails and ledges to the pass.

Net Elevation Gain

The elevation gain from Lake Louise to the Pass is about 3,900 ft.

Time

It is a long day to get to the pass from Lake Louise via this route. Leave yourself all day, because you certainly do not want to be mucking around on the ledges on the west side of Lefroy in the dark. Small, experienced parties traveling light have recorded times in the neighborhood of seven to eight hours for the whole trip up to the pass; times for the descent would be somewhat less.

Approach

From Lake Louise, follow the Plain of Six Glaciers Teahouse trail as for the Death Trap route, descending to the Victoria Glacier a little ways past the teahouse. It is easier to gain the Victoria Glacier at a point before the teahouse where the trail comes close to the glacier — the trade-off is that more time is spent on the glacier, and less on the highly developed Parks Canada trail beside it.

Whichever way you get onto the Victoria Glacier, cross it to the south to the Lefroy Glacier, then head toward, and begin climbing up, the largest scree cone coming out of a large gully/chimney on the east face of Lefroy. This is the largest such feature on this face of Lefroy. It is difficult to see the ledges, or the cairn which marks their beginning from the scree approach itself; if you are on the largest scree cone, proceed on faith that the cairn is there. As you near the top of the scree, there are some steeper steps of rock on the right; these can be climbed directly or bypassed on the left (recommended). Very near the top of the scree slope, a cairn identifies the start of the ledge heading north. The ledge itself is punctuated by gullies and drainages which provide small scrambling challenges with very exciting exposure; some groups may want to travel roped across the length of the ledge. The ledge reaches the north ridge of Lefroy and turns the corner onto the west face at grid reference 503922 and at an elevation of 8,060 ft.

Once on the west face, the terrain opens up and the exposure is reduced dramatically, and more options for travel are presented. Various cairned trails lead across this slope and toward the pass, each presenting periodic scrambling and continuous route-finding challenges. When in doubt, it is probably better to stay high rather than low. This section of the approach is long and involved, including almost 2,000 ft. of elevation gain to the pass. Anticipate three or more hours for this section of the approach alone.

If using this route as a descent from the pass, reverse the above description. The greatest potential route-finding problem is going to be turning the corner onto the east face at the proper place and locating the beginning of the ledge. Make a descending traverse across the west slopes of Lefroy from the pass, watching for cairns, and aiming for the broadest scree ledges directly above the Death Trap. Gradually work your way forward along a ledge, which narrows progressively until you find yourself just above a significant drop-off. A prominent gendarme should be visible on the ridge of Lefroy 200 feet above . From this point the route is more obvious: head for marks on the rock. Turn the corner at grid reference 502922 and you should find yourself on the traverse ledge noted in the ascent description. You can confirm your position by noting a series of unusually distinct, parallel and finely layered limestone strata on the right wall of the ledge. Once on the ledge, continue south, then descend scree to the Lefroy Glacier.

FACILITIES

The Hut and Accommodation

With Mt. Victoria as a backdrop, and built from the stones of Abbot Pass, the hut is a magnificent sight; the building still stands in its original form and probably will for the next century. The hut sleeps 20 people comfortably with new sleeping arrangements on the upper level. On the main floor is the custodian's quarters (the B.C. Room) and a small accommodation area (the Alberta Room).

Heat Source

There is a coal-burning stove for heat (coal stoves are very efficient when operated properly, and a pain when they are not — please read the directions in the front of this book). The coal supply is found behind the hut in barrels, or under the walkway of the outhouse, accessible via a top hatch. Please burn as little wood as possible, as it is supplied for kindling only. A good alternative to burning wood is using Zip brand charcoal starter cubes with the coal.

Cooking and Lighting

The Huts Committee is in the process of changing the white gas Coleman stoves and lanterns to propane - check with the reservations office for details.

Tools

There are snow shovels and a small hatchet for splitting the kindling.

Water Supply

Water comes primarily from snow melt available year-round just outside the hut, but in mid - to late summer a small run-off from a pipe on the west slopes of Lefroy towards Ringrose Peak may be used as well.

Grey Water

A screened grey water pit is located just in front and to the west of the outhouse steps. It is most convenient to screen the grey water as it is running out of the sinks. Food bits should be burned in the coal stove or packed out as garbage.

Outhouses

The outhouse is located 10m northwest of the hut on an elevated platform. The Abbot Pass outhouse is a barrel fly-out system with a separate drain-away urinal which should be used whenever possible. Do not dispose of any unnecessary waste in the outhouse or urinal.

OPPORTUNITIES

The Abbot Pass Hut is used today, as it was in the beginning, as a base for climbing on Mts. Victoria and Lefroy. The routes from the pass are classic moderate alpine outings and are "must do" routes for locals and visitors alike. During the summer when the Lake O'Hara bus is operating, the hut is popular and can be completely full on weekends; in the spring and fall the number of visitors drops off radically, and winter usage is rarely even a blip on the statistics graph.

Mountaineering

There are essentially two mountaineering routes from the pass: the South-East Ridge of the south summit of Victoria, and the West Face of Lefroy. The former is one of the most elegant ridge routes in the Rockies, while the latter gives excellent snow or ice climbing of a moderate standard. Both routes take you to the top of impressive 11,000+ ft. peaks, give excellent views and are highly recommended. It is also possible to traverse the Mt. Victoria massif from the pass. This is a less popular, and certainly more committing outing than either of the other two routes.

Information on these routes can be found in ***Selected Alpine Climbs in the Canadian Rockies*** and ***The Rocky Mountains of Canada – South.***

The Fay Hut

HISTORY

The Fay Hut was built in 1927 as a base for climbing in the Valley of the Ten Peaks and, although it is predated by the Elizabeth Parker and the Abbot Pass Huts, it has the distinction of being the first hut built or operated by the ACC. Abbot Pass and Elizabeth Parker were both built by the Canadian Pacific Railroad and were taken over by the ACC some time later.

Charles E. Fay was the founder of the Appalachian Mountain Club and the American Alpine Club. He was the long-time editor of two mountaineering periodicals and from 1890 to 1930 made 25 trips to the Canadian Rockies. He was an excellent climber in his day, and participated in the first ascents of Mt. Victoria and Mt. Lefroy, among others. He was recognized as an honorary member of the alpine clubs of England, France, Italy and Canada.

The Fay Hut was maintained and operated by the ACC until 1972 when it was turned over to Kootenay National Park; a tree had fallen through the roof nine years earlier and the Club could not afford the $2,000 required to repair it. In 1991, in an ironic shift of philosophy, the Park returned the hut to the Club rather than invest the $11,000 that it then required for renovations. Through an enormous effort by the ACC and the Rocky Mountain Section of the Club in 1991, the hut has been returned to excellent condition.

LOCATION

General Location

The hut is located on a treed bench above Prospectors Valley and south of The Valley of the Ten Peaks, in Kootenay National Park.

Map References

The hut is located on 82N/8 (Lake Louise). The first 10 km of the Prospectors Valley trail is located on 82N1 (Mount Goodsir).

Grid Reference

The hut is at 553791, and is labelled "Cabin" on 82N/8 (Lake Louise).

Altitude

The hut sits at 6,915 ft. (2,108m).

ACCESS

Prospector's Valley Approach

Net Elevation Gain

From the Marble Canyon parking lot, the trail rises 2,000 ft. to the hut, 1,500 of it in the last 2 km.

Time

Four hours is pretty standard for this approach.

Approach

Start the hike from the Marble Canyon parking lot, 6.5 km west of the Banff National Park/Kootenay National Park boundary on the Banff-Radium Highway 93 (not to be confused with the Icefields Parkway Highway 93). The route follows the Tokumm Creek Trail along the east bank of the river for 10 km to a signed junction for the Fay Hut. This first 10-km stretch presents very few route finding challenges, as it starts on an old access road and follows a defined trail for its length. At the trail junction, the route to the hut turns north (right) and begins to gain elevation. After about two kilometres and 1,500 ft. of elevation gain from the junction, the trail breaks through a steep gully which presents the most challenging part of the approach. Scramble up trails on scree and the rock of the gully itself to reach the top of the trail in about 50m. There is a length of rope hanging down the steepest part of the gully, but it is usually not required. At the top of the gully, the trail levels off and the hut is found in the trees to the right (east).

WINTER ACCESS

The winter route follows the same terrain as the summer trail, with a few small deviations. Hut users should refer to Chic Scott's ***Ski Trails In the Canadian Rockies*** for a complete description.

FACILITIES

The hut and accommodation

The hut is a beautiful one room log cabin with a large two-tiered sleeping platform for 12 people.

Heat Source

The hut is heated by a wood-burning stove. The wood is stored just outside of the front door.

Cooking

There are two two-burner Coleman white gas stoves for cooking and sufficient cooking and eating utensils for the capacity of the hut.

Lighting

Coleman white gas lanterns are provided for light.

Water Supply

There is a creek 100m south of the hut. In the winter it may be necessary to melt snow.

Grey Water

There is a ground sump for grey water disposal 10m south of the front door of the hut. In the winter it may be necessary to excavate the sump.

Outhouse

The outhouse is on a barrel fly-out system. Please refer to the instructions in the front of the book, and change the barrels when they are full. Please do not put any unnecessary garbage in the outhouse. The outhouse is located 25m west of the hut, by the trail down to Tokumm Creek.

Garbage

Burn paper garbage and food scraps in the wood stove and pack all other garbage out with you.

OPPORTUNITIES

Mountaineering

The hut was originally built to facilitate climbs in The Valley of the Ten Peaks, but since the erection of high altitude huts in the area it has been used far less for this purpose. Between 1962 and 1983 the climbs in the Ten Peaks area were commonly approached from the Graham Cooper Hut and in 1983 that hut was replaced by the larger Neil Colgan Hut. It is still possible to make ascents in the area from this base below treeline, and Mts. Little, Fay and Quadra are the most common. Complete route information can be found in ***Selected Alpine Climbs in the Canadian Rockies,*** and ***The Rocky Mountains of Canada – South.***

Backcountry Skiing

The trip up Tokumm Creek to the hut itself is an excellent ski, with great scenery and an interesting little bit of climbing up the slope at the end. To continue up to the Neil Colgan Hut is a great tour as well, but can be very adventurous if the conditions are not ideal. Finishing the trip to Kaufmann Lakes (the turn-off on the trail at the 10-kilometre marker is most of the way there) is a good objective as well. The best source of information for these trips is ***Ski Trails in the Canadian Rockies.***

The Neil Colgan Hut

HISTORY

Second to the scene of Lake Louise set against the backdrop of Mt. Victoria, Moraine Lake is perhaps the most photographed and best known mountain scene in the Canadian Rockies. The area behind the first row of peaks which can be seen from the lake provides excellent alpine climbing on snow and ice routes, and makes an ideal location for a high altitude climbing hut. The area saw its first hut in 1964 when the Calgary Mountain Club erected a hut at the top of the couloir between peaks 3 and 3$^1/_2$. This original hut was named for Graham Cooper, who died while descending after the construction of the hut. The hut was in a poor position, however, because it encouraged use of the couloir as an access route to the hut. By the 1980s the couloir had seen many rockfall accidents and several fatalities. The hut was dismantled and replaced by the Neil Colgan Hut in 1983.

Neil Colgan was a warden in Banff National Park when he died from injuries sustained in a horse accident in the backcountry. The hut was largely funded by his family in his name.

LOCATION

General Location

The hut sits on the Continental Divide in a col between Mts. Little and Bowlen (peaks 2 and 3 of the Valley of the Ten Peaks). The hut is the highest permanent structure in Canada, edging out the Abbot Pass Hut by about 100 ft.

Map References

The hut is on 82N/8 (Lake Louise). The approaches from Moraine Lake are on this map as well; the approach from Tokumm Creek and the Fay Hut begins on map 82N/1 (Mt. Goodsir).

Grid Reference

The hut is located at 568830 on 82N/8 (Lake Louise).

Altitude

The hut sits at 9,700 ft. (2,940m).

ACCESS

There are three common routes to the hut: two technical routes from Moraine Lake, and the more circuitous route up Tokumm Creek via the Fay Hut. ***All routes to the Neil Colgan Hut require glacier travel and crevasse rescue skills and proper equipment.*** In the winter, only the Fay Hut route is recommended, and then only in times of low avalanche danger.

In the past, particularly in the days of the Graham Cooper Hut, the 3-3½ couloir was used as an approach to the area. However, the rock in the Valley of the Ten Peaks area is generally quite rank (some people will tell you that this is where the Rockies got its reputation for lousy rock), and the decaying walls that tower above this couloir regularly send debris screaming through it with no warning. As a result this route has been the scene of several fatalities. This route is far too dangerous to be recommended as an access to the area, or even a climb in its own right. Do not go here.

Perren Route

The amount of technical climbing required to get up this route has been lessened significantly with the installation of bolts and chains at the hardest sections, but it is still not to be taken lightly. The wall is steep, and remember that the packs and boots you are likely to be wearing on your way to this hut will make the climbing harder.

Net elevation gain

From Moraine Lake the route gains 3,500 ft. to the hut.

Time

Five to seven hours for this approach is standard. There is a great deal of hiking uphill through scree and over ledges which could be harder to follow and more work if there is snow on the ground. There is also a formidable section of rock climbing involved, and climbing with heavy packs or setting up to haul them will also take time. Gauge your own ability accordingly.

Gear

You will need a set of quickdraws to clip the bolts and links of the chain as you Batman past the 5.7 sections, a lead rope, and of course, helmets. A few wired stoppers and a couple of camming devices may add some peace of mind in a couple of places.

Approach

Begin the approach by hiking along the north shore of Moraine Lake to the creek which flows from the Wenkchemna, Glacier and the end of a boardwalk. From here either plow straight through the cold water or head up the creek to the north for 50m to a log-and-cable crossing. If you opt for the water, it is advisable to wear an old pair of runners or sandals (maybe even wear them from the car) and carry a ski pole or other such implement, as the water is fast. The log crossing is a good option unless, of course, you fall in. The logs are slimy, the cables are loose, and depending on the time of day and season, the logs may be under water. It is highly recommended to wear crampons for this crossing.

From the south side of the creek head along a trail through the forest for five to ten minutes until it opens up into a boulder field. Work your way through the large boulders and up a talus slope, trending left, toward the base of a large quartzite buttress. A good trail runs along the base of quartzite ledges to the top of the talus slope, where it is possible to break left onto a well-defined trail and ledge system. The trail ascends over ledges and trails toward two obvious cliff bands. At the first cliffband, follow a line which scrambles through a gully; at the second cliffband, the technical climbing begins. Put on the rope and begin climbing a few metres from the extreme left side of the cliff where several pitons and a chain mark the route. Also marking the route is an orange triangle/arrow thing painted on the rock at the bottom stance — an interesting souvenir from the old days. The route is easy to follow, and involves three separate pitches: the first is the steepest and hardest; the second, a traverse to the right (following bolts) to a large ledge; and the third a less technical, but more run-out pitch to the base of the glacier. There are several ways to climb the final pitch, the easiest of which begins about 25m along the large ledge, and slightly past a fixed anchor which is used for descending the lower wall. Climb a slab just left of a small groove, and then step right into a large groove. Trend left on good ledges which take you to the top of the cliff and a fixed anchor (25m). It is a good idea to familiarize yourself with the descent anchors on your way up, particularly if you plan to return this way. One rope is sufficient to rappel this line, but just. Don't try it with a rope less than 50 metres long.

The Perren Route itself tops out at the glacier at grid reference 572838. It is a good idea to keep this reference number handy in the event you are descending this route in poor visibility. From the top of the rock climbing, proceed up the glacier in a southerly direction toward Mt. Little, until it is possible to gain a ridge of snow on the glacier and contour across the north slopes of that mountain to the hut at the Little-Bowlen col.

Schiesser Ledges

Net Elevation Gain

From Moraine Lake the route gains 3,500 ft. to the hut.

Time

This approach is about the same as the Perren Route – allow yourself five to seven hours for the trip.

Approach

The route begins by following the north shore of Moraine Lake to the end of the boardwalk. Stay on the north side of the creek following a good trail until you reach a swampy meadow. Cross the swampy meadow to a terminal moraine which has a trail on its left flank. Follow this trail to the base of a large crescent-shaped lateral moraine. The key to this section is identifying the crescent-shaped moraine at the base of Peak 3½, and following the trail on its crest. This trail will take you to the base of the 3½-4 couloir. The ledges and small cliff bands to the left of the couloir are the Schiesser Ledges route. Ascend the scree slopes to the left of the lower couloir to a point where you must take to the rock. The beginning of the route is obvious when you find it, as it is marked with a large splotch of red paint. Continue up the ledges and over scree to the col, following red paint splotches and keeping well left of the couloir. At the col, the route contours around the southwest side of Mt. Bowlen to the Little-Bowlen Col, and the Neil Colgan Hut.

Notes: This route has some objective hazard from rockfall. Also, the chains, cables and anchors which are found on this route are old and should not be trusted.

Fay Hut Route

This is the longest, but certainly the least technical of the three approaches to the Colgan Hut.

Net Elevation Gain

From the Fay Hut, the elevation gain is about 2,800 ft. to the Neil Colgan Hut. From the Fay Hut trail head, the elevation gain is a little over 4,800 ft. to the Neil Colgan Hut.

Time

It takes a pretty big effort to reach the Neil Colgan Hut from the road in a single day via this approach; total traveling time is going to be in the seven to ten hour range. Either take it easy and spend a night in the cozy Fay Hut, breaking the trip up into two days, or start early, have lunch at the Fay Hut and push on to the Colgan Hut in the afternoon.

Approach

Refer to the Fay Hut approach to get there. From the Fay Hut, proceed in a northwesterly direction over faint trails to the mouth of an obvious canyon. Do not proceed up the canyon. On the north side of the canyon, and several hundred feet higher than its mouth, is a large open plateau which takes you to the moraine and the glacier. To gain this plateau, cross the creek at the mouth of the canyon and follow a faint trail which takes you left of the canyon, around an orange buttress of rock and onto a treed slope. Ascend the treed slope on a faint trail to the open plateau above it. Follow the moraine and glacier in a north-northeasterly direction toward the Little-Bowlen col. Approach the col from the Mt. Little side, contouring across its west slopes to the col and the hut.

FACILITIES

The Hut and Accommodation

The hut is a one-room building with bunks for 18 people (16 in the winter), a large table and benches, and a long counter opposite the bunks for cooking. Sleeping 18 people on the bunks is not a problem; however, the storage of gear and cooking arrangements can be a little tight when the hut is at capacity. Good organization of personal gear is important.

Heat Source

The hut is well insulated and stays warm in the winter with body heat, the lanterns on and a bunch of cooking happening, but there is no wood-burning stove.

Cooking

The hut is well equipped with cooking and eating utensils for 18 and two Coleman white-gas stoves.

Lighting

Coleman white-gas lanterns are provided for lighting.

Water Supply

Run-off from Mt. Little is often available behind the hut by mid-summer, but you should be prepared to melt snow. The hut is situated on a col between two glaciers, so finding enough snow to melt is not a concern.

Grey Water

A grey water disposal site at the Neil Colgan Hut is not presently designated. It is recommended that strained water be dumped into the porous rock field which disperses it. Strained food scraps from the grey water should be packed out as garbage.

Outhouse

The outhouse is on a barrel fly-out system. Please refer to the instructions in the front of the book, and change the barrels when they are full. Please do not put any unnecessary garbage in the outhouse. The outhouse is located 30m northwest (in front) of the hut. There is also a urinal adjacent to the toilet; this is for urine only.

Garbage

All garbage and unused food must be packed out from the hut.

OPPORTUNITIES

Mountaineering

This site, at the col between Mts. Little and Bowlen, is a convenient location for climbing. The peaks of The Valley of the Ten Peaks are all over 10,000 ft, and the hut, at 9,700 ft, is an ideal base for bagging these summits. It is standard to climb a number of peaks in a day, and it is not uncommon to stop back at the hut for lunch on the porch, or another cup of coffee between summits.

The routes accessible from the hut range from walk-ups of Mts. Little and Bowlen, just outside the hut, to the north face ice routes on Mt. Fay. The snow and ice routes in the area are very good, but the rock is abysmal. In fact if you came up the Perren Route to the hut, you have done all of the worthwhile rock climbing in the area. The north face routes on Mt. Fay are classic summer alpine ice outings, and are the biggest attraction of the area. Information on these routes can be found in ***Selected Alpine Climbs in the Canadian Rockies*** and in ***The Rocky Mountains of Canada – South.***

The Castle Mountain Hut

HISTORY

The Castle Mountain Hut began as a leftover. In 1964 the Calgary Mountain Club financed a project to build a high altitude climbing hut in the Valley of the Ten Peaks. The six-person bivouac shelter, which was to become the Graham Cooper Hut, was designed and built by a construction technology class at the Southern Alberta Institute of Technology in Calgary. Because the hut was quite small, and did not provide enough of a project for the class, a second identical hut, with no predetermined destination, was produced at the same time. This second hut sat for three years before it was erected at its present site on Goat Plateau, halfway up Castle Mountain, and has long outlasted its sister hut which was replaced by the Neil Colgan Hut in 1983.

Upon its completion in July, 1967, the hut was turned over to Banff National Park. Operation of the hut was turned over to the Alpine Club of Canada in 1987.

LOCATION

General Location

On "Goat Plateau," halfway up Castle Mountain. The hut can actually be seen from the Trans-Canada Highway as a small white speck near the edge of the cliff on the sixth buttress from the east.

Map Reference

The hut, the approach and the whole of Castle Mountain are found on map 82O/5 (Castle Mountain).

Grid Reference

The hut is located at 743836 on 82O/5. There is a cabin labelled on the map, but it is incorrectly positioned.

Altitude

The hut sits at 7,850 ft. (2,390m).

ACCESS

Fire Lookout Approach

This is the standard approach to the hut, although the Rockbound Lake approach is used more often by parties climbing Eisenhower Tower and not staying at the hut. The Fire Lookout approach, however, is a more technical climb and may therefore appeal less to some.

Net elevation gain

From the parking lot to the hut is approximately 3,000 ft. of elevation gain. This is the same for the Rockbound Lake approach — it's a pretty stiff grunt by either route.

Time

Standard time from the highway to the hut is three hours. This time will vary, of course, between parties. Expect to take slightly longer your first time up this approach, as route-finding can be time consuming. The record for a trip from the hut to the Banff liquor store and back is 2 hours 50 minutes.

Approach:

From the Castle Junction on the 1A Highway, drive west for 4.8 km to a paved parking lot and the signed trailhead to the Fire Lookout. Four kilometres of steady uphill hiking on an old fire road and trails takes you pretty close to the treeline and the site of the old fire lookout. With a commanding view of the entire valley, it is easy to see the logic in choosing this locale for the lookout.

From here, a number of trails continue up the slope in an easterly direction. The most advantageous trail is one which follows the left side of a rocky gully before crossing the gully at some boulders a few hundred metres up the slope. Once on the other side of the gully, follow more faint trails which switchback up toward the lower cliffband. Getting through this lower cliffband is both the technical and route-finding crux of this approach. Many different (and more difficult) lines through here have been attempted by parties which did not locate the "diagonal break" through the cliffband. The diagonal break is the key to this approach — it certainly has the easiest climbing, and is not too hard to find if you know what you are looking for. The correct break to ascend is one which diagonals upward to the right and is about 20m high. A very defined trail leads straight up to the base of it, and there is very little which looks climbable to its right (you end up in a large gross gully). If this does not seem like the piece of rock you are looking at, DON'T go up it. There are retreat slings from past parties in different places on this section of cliff; don't let these sucker you up a bad line! In fact, if there are slings on the route you are looking at, it is probably wrong. The diagonal break itself is not difficult climbing (low 5th class), but if you take into account overnight packs, big boots and unfamiliar terrain, the commitment increases dramatically. It is highly recommended that you carry a rope and a rack on this approach to belay on this section.

Climber in the diagonal break

Once above the diagonal break you will find trails and ledges leading up into a large gully. Follow these, and the small cairns which mark them. These trails eventually round a buttress in the gully and take you into a parallel gully on the right. This portion of the trail occasionally gives parties some grief, particularly early in the year when snow remains in the gullies, covering some of the trail. Follow the cairns carefully.

The right hand gully takes you up through more trails and ledges to a slightly more involved scrambling section higher up. There are many possible routes through this scrambling section, some much better than others. You can follow cairns through much of it, until it gets a little steeper, at which point you have to resort to following trails on the ledges and worn sections on the rock. At any rate, the scrambling here is easier than any of the climbing through the diagonal break.

This gully eventually deposits you on the Goat Plateau, half way up Castle Mountain. From this point, follow the trails across Goat Plateau to the east for a couple of hundred metres to the hut.

Rockbound Lake Approach

This approach will appeal to those looking for a less technical route to the hut than the Fire Lookout approach, but while the climbing is technically easier, there is still a fair amount of scrambling to get onto Goat Plateau.

Time and Net Elevation Gain

This is going to be approximately the same as for the Fire Lookout Approach; about three hours and 3,000 ft.

Approach

The approach hike begins at the Rockbound Lake trailhead about 50m east of Castle Junction. Follow the main trail for 4 to 5 km to where the trail rounds the base of the Castle Mountain and begins to head northwest. Here you will find a section of the trail which is braided and swampy for most of the season just before it levels out toward Rockbound Lake itself. Approximately 70m past this braided section is a faint trail heading off to the left from the main trail. Follow this faint trail along the forested crest of the ridge leading to the cliffs at the southeast extremity of Castle Mountain. Scramble up easy ground to an obvious ledge which traverses back around to the highway side of the

Traverse Ledge

mountain. The trail on this ledge is well worn and easy to identify. Follow this trail around the corner (less than 100m) and scramble up more ledges (somewhat more exposed) toward an obvious large gully which takes you to Goat Plateau. The best trail to follow along the plateau to the hut is one which is high up on the plateau, at the base of the upper cliff. It might not be a bad idea to wear a helmet for this portion of the approach.

Some literature, including the first edition of the ACC Facilities Directory, has suggested that an alternate route to the Goat Plateau is to traverse right instead of left around the lower buttress to another gully. This way takes you to the plateau from the Rockbound Lake side of the mountain rather than the highway side. This route is much more dangerous in both the traverse and the gully itself (actually it is quite gross), and it puts you on the far side of the mountain from where you want to go, be it the hut or Eisenhower Tower. Anyone suggesting this route to you should be treated with suspicion.

WINTER ACCESS

This is a summer hut. Like all of the ACC huts, the Castle Mountain Hut is technically open all year round, but the nature of the approaches, the attraction of the area (almost exclusively rock climbing) and the humble facilities all but preclude winter visits. If you were to head up here in the snow, you would need to be very cautious of avalanche slopes, both on the approaches and from above. Check with Wardens for snow conditions.

FACILITIES

The Hut and Accommodation

Perched 3,000 ft. above the Bow Valley, with views that span from Banff to Lake Louise, the attraction of this hut is most definitely the setting rather than the building. The hut itself is modest, one of the most modest in the ACC chain in fact, but serves precisely the need in this location. There are foam mattresses for six people (there are four bunks and the boards between them pull out to make a sleeping space for six).

Heat Source

The hut does not have a wood-burning stove, but is small and well insulated and becomes very warm from body heat, lanterns and cooking.

Cooking

This hut is well supplied for small parties with a two-burner Coleman white gas stove and sufficient cooking and eating supplies for six. Don't go to this hut expecting to be able to prepare elaborate meals, but for pasta and cereal, you're styling.

Lighting

A Coleman white gas lantern is provided for light.

Tools

The hut has a couple of brooms and a shovel (in case you get snowed in).

Water Supply

The standard water source is the small creek at the top of the Fire Lookout approach. It flows in some manner for most months, and dries up completely only late in the season during very dry summers.

Grey Water

A grey water disposal site at the Castle Mountain Hut is not presently designated. It is recommended that strained water be dumped into porous rock fields in the vicinity of the hut to disperse it. Strained food scraps from the grey water should be packed out as garbage.

Outhouse

The outhouse is located 40m to the east, at the edge of the cliff.

Garbage

All garbage, including unused food, must be packed out from the hut.

OPPORTUNITIES

The main attraction at the Castle Mountain Hut is rock climbing. You may run into a little snow on the top of the mountain on your way to the descent gully early in the year, but that's going to be it; leave your crampons and big boots at home!

Alpine Rock Climbing

The rock on Castle Mountain varies from excellent to absolute garbage, and most routes are going to have at least a taste of everything in between. Most of the routes are located on the upper cliff band, but there is excellent potential for a variety of climbs on the lower walls as well. *Ultra Brewers* on the lower wall has two of the best pitches on natural protection to be found anywhere on limestone in the province, and *Brewer Buttress* on the upper wall is quite simply the best long rock climb of its grade (5.6) in the Bow Valley.

The routes are typically Grade II or Grade III, follow the most obvious features, and incorporate a wide range of rock quality.

The best information on the standard routes on the cliff is found in ***Selected Alpine Climbs*** and ***The Rocky Mountains of Canada – South;*** the latter describes more of the routes on the upper wall, while the former describes the routes in greater detail. New route information is recorded in the hut log book.

Sport Climbing

In addition to traditional rock climbing, the Castle Mountain Hut also gives access to one excellent sport climb. A single pitch straight down the lower cliff from the hut itself provides excellent climbing in a stunning "Verdon-esque" position. The approach involves rappelling from bolts at the edge of the cliff to a second bolted station 25m down the wall. The route is named *Rim Job,* and goes at 5.11a.

The Stanley Mitchell Hut

HISTORY

Along with A.O. Wheeler and Elizabeth Parker, Stanley Mitchell was responsible for founding the Alpine Club of Canada in 1906, and from 1907 to 1930 he served as its Secretary Treasurer. He had a great reputation as a gentleman among his fellow founders and the executive of the Club, as well as the members he met at the Club House in Banff. He died in 1940, shortly after the hut which bears his name was completed.

The Little Yoho Valley has long had a reputation as an excellent alpine climbing area as well as a magnificent skiing area. The Canadian military used the area during the summer of 1943 as a training site for mountaineering techniques. From 1954 to the mid-70s Hans Gmoser used the hut as a lodge for a new ski touring operation — a company which eventually became Canadian Mountain Holidays.

The hut has changed little in 56 years, with the exception of renovations, the latest of which in the summer of 1994 saw new windows, new furniture and improved sleeping arrangements upstairs. The hut is presently in excellent condition, a comfortable facility set in beautiful meadow and mountain terrain, and a fine memorial to one of the Club's founders.

LOCATION

General Location

The hut sits in a small meadow not far from the base of The President, in the Little Yoho Valley, Yoho National Park, B.C.

Map References

The hut is found on the bottom right hand corner of map 82N/10 (Blaeberry River), the parking lot and trailhead on the upper left corner of 82N/8 (Lake Louise), and the middle part of the trail on the lower left corner of 82N/9 (Hector Lake). It is also advisable to carry 82N/7 (Golden) if you wish to climb the President and the

Vice President. For your travelling convenience, the critical areas of the above four maps have been reproduced onto one sheet: ***Touring the Wapta Icefields,*** by Murray Toft. This map is definitely recommended.

Grid Reference

The hut is located at 303081 on 82N/10 (Blaeberry River) and the Toft map.

Altitude

The hut sits at 6,825 ft. (2,060m).

SUMMER ACCESS

The two common approaches to the Stanley Mitchell Hut are the Little Yoho Valley Trail and the Iceline Trail. Both originate at the Takakkaw Falls parking lot and follow well-developed National Park trail systems. It is more common to approach the hut on the former trail, and to hike the Iceline on the descent, to avoid the immediate gruelling uphill of this trail. Descending this way you also hike toward, rather than away from, the spectacular scenery the Iceline affords.

Little Yoho Valley Approach

This is the most common way of getting to the hut. The trails are well developed and maintained, the route is well graded, and (including a few short optional diversions), very scenic. This is also the standard route to the hut in the winter.

Net elevation gain

From the Takakkaw Falls parking lot, the trail rises about 1,700 ft. (about 520m).

Time

The standard hiking time in the summer is three to four hours, but be prepared to add to that if you don't do a lot of backpacking or if you have all of your kids' stuff as well as your own on your back. Because a lot of parties use this hut as one of their first backpacking trips and as an introduction to backcountry adventures, it can be underestimated.

Approach

Follow the Yoho Valley Road (begins 3.7 km east of Field, B.C.) to the Takakkaw Falls parking lot at its end (13 km from the #1 Highway). Park at the most northerly point, and begin hiking on the Little Yoho Valley and Twin Falls trail (signed). The trail is mostly level for the first 4 km or so, and really begins gaining elevation after passing Laughing Falls. At Laughing Falls you will come to a trail junction which leads to Twin Falls to the right, and the Little Yoho Valley to the left; keep left here, and begin up the switchbacks. There is another trail junction for Marpole Lake about half a kilometre before reaching the top of the Laughing Falls Hill. Stay left on the trail which continues to climb the hill. half a kilometre further, and pretty much at the top of the elevation gain, you will come to another junction indicating the Whaleback trail to your right, and the Little Yoho Valley to the left; go left here, and then to the right at the next junction which is less than a 100m further. In approximately another 3 km you will come to an open meadow and the Stanley Mitchell Hut.

Iceline Trail

This trail provides spectacular views of Takakkaw Falls and the glaciers beyond; you can picture where the Scott Duncan hut lies north of Mt. Daly on the southern end of the Waputik Icefield. This trail is more commonly used descending from the hut, making a great loop trail.

Net elevation gain

The net gain is much the same as for the Yoho Valley Trail. This trail does actually gain an extra couple of hundred feet before descending to the hut, but the real issue is that all of the uphill is packed into the first few gruelling kilometres.

Time

About the same as the Little Yoho Valley trail, perhaps a little longer.

Approach

Drive up the Yoho Valley Road as described above. Leave your car at a parking lot beside the Whiskey Jack Hostel, just before the falls. Climb the trail up the hillside above, through the forest to the left of a giant avalanche slide path. After 1 km there is a junction for a side trip to Hidden Lake to the left, and a couple of hundred metres further, a junction for Yoho Pass and Lake to the left. Keep right at both of these intersections. The trail continues rising, then levels out and follows very well-developed trails on old moraine on the northeast side of the President range, before dropping down to the Little Yoho River and the Stanley Mitchell Hut.

WINTER ACCESS

A summary of winter access routes is given below. This information describes the character and difficulty of the undertaking, but is inadequate for planning or carrying out the trips themselves. Please refer to ***Ski Trails in the Canadian Rockies,*** or ***Summits and Icefields*** by Chic Scott for complete access information.

Two routes are commonly used to access the hut in winter: the Little Yoho Valley approach, which gives access from the highway in a one-day push, and the less common multi-day route across the des Poilus Glacier from the Wapta Icefields. Both routes are serious undertakings, and as a result this hut is used much less in the winter than in the summer months.

Little Yoho Valley

The road to Takakkaw Falls is not plowed in winter, and must be skied. After arriving at the falls, the route follows the one taken in summer.

Net elevation gain

The ascent from the highway to the hut is approximately 2,200 ft. (675m).

Time

Allow a full day for this approach. You may split the trip into two days, with a bivouac at the campground cook shelter just past the falls.

Approach

The route follows the road to Takakkaw Falls and the summer hiking trail to the hut. The trail signs may be completely under snow, and the final stretch to the hut may be difficult to follow if a trail has not been broken or if the sun goes down. The route is described in full detail by Chic Scott in ***Ski Trails in the Canadian Rockies*** (pages 135-137) and ***Summits and Icefields*** (pages 125-126).

The Yoho Traverse

This is a major, multi-day ski tour with a couple of variations. You can begin at either the Bow or Peyto Hut, or the highway. It is common to push through to the Stanley Mitchell Hut in a day from the Bow Hut, but many parties camp out one night in a snow cave on the des Poilus Glacier. The summary description below assumes a start at the Bow Hut.

Net Elevation Gain

There is a net elevation loss coming off the Wapta Icefield, but there are a lot of ups and downs along the way. From the Bow Hut you will have gained about 2,700 ft., and lost about 3,600 ft. by the time you get to the Stanley Mitchell Hut.

Time

The route is often done in a day from Bow, but many parties plan on two days. A night out should be planned for, even if not anticipated.

Approach

The route crosses the Wapta Icefield to the west through the Rhondda – Mt. Gordon Pass and across the southeast slopes of Mt. Collie before descending south onto the des Poilus Glacier. Pass Isolated Peak on the east side, and descend its south slopes to the hut. This route is described in detail in Chic Scott's ***Summits and Icefields*** and ***Ski Trails in the Canadian Rockies*** guides as The Yoho Traverse.

FACILITIES

The Hut and Accommodation

A gorgeous log cabin sitting in a beautiful alpine meadow, the Stanley Mitchell Hut is one of the most attractive and picturesque of the Alpine Club's huts. There is accommodation for 28 people in the summer and 22 in the winter in a small room downstairs and the entire upstairs loft. The kitchen area is in a separate room, and the whole hut is bright and open thanks to the recent window renovations.

Heat Source

The hut is heated by an air-tight wood stove in the common area; the wood supply is in a woodshed behind the hut.

Cooking

Three Coleman white gas stoves in the kitchen, as well as cooking and eating utensils for about 30 people.

Lighting

There are three Coleman white gas lanterns are provided.

Tools

Saws, axes and shovels are kept in the woodshed or in the small sleeping room downstairs.

Water Supply

A small spring-fed creek running through the meadow 60m south of the hut provides the water supply. The spring is below treeline, so it is advisable to boil or treat it before drinking. In the winter you can dig down to the creek or melt snow for water.

Grey Water

There is a ground sump behind the hut, visible from the kitchen window. In the summer it may be necessary to excavate the sump.

Outhouse

The two outhouses are located about 30m behind the hut — one on each side.

Garbage

Burn all paper garbage and food scraps and pack out all other garbage and unused food.

OPPORTUNITIES

Mountaineering and Scrambling

The big draw of the area is the President and the Vice President. The routes from the col between them are excellent moderate mountaineering challenges which see a fair number of beginners brought along. The

Vice President also offers a very good snow and ice route on the north face. The North Ridge and East Face of Mt. McArthur to the northwest are also very good alpine outings.

Besides the President and Vice President, the other peaks in the area are primarily scrambling outings. Some of the most common objectives are Mt. Kerr, Mt. Polinger, Kiwetinok Peak and Isolated Peak. There is also very good scrambling along Whaleback Mountain. Information on these routes can be found in ***Selected Alpine Climbs in the Canadian Rockies,*** and ***The Rocky Mountains of Canada – South.***

Ice Climbing

The hut is not exactly a base for lots of different ice routes, but a couple of harder to access climbs are best done from here. Twin Falls is a 22 km grunt from the highway, or about a 7 km ski from the hut. Takakkaw Falls is almost equidistant from the highway and the hut, but if you start from the hut the approach is downhill, and so is the ski back to the highway. There are some unclimbed smears on the northeast face of the President which occasionally form early in the year, and may be climbed someday. Information on these routes can be found in ***Waterfall Ice Climbs in the Canadian Rockies.***

Day Hiking

The hiking on established trails in the vicinity of the hut is very good, with interesting trips back down the valley toward Twin Falls (such as the Whaleback trail and the Marpole Lake trail) as well as up past the hut toward Kiwetinok Pass. Refer to ***The Canadian Rockies Trail Guide*** and ***The Wonder of Yoho*** for more information on these and other trails.

Backcountry Skiing

Chic Scott in ***Summits and Icefields*** raves about the Little Yoho Valley in the winter, referring to both the skiing terrain and the warmth and atmosphere at the Stanley Mitchell Hut. According to Chic, and he would know, the valley, with its perfect terrain, excellent snow and ski runs which end at the back door of the hut is the "Gem of the Rockies". What more needs to be said?

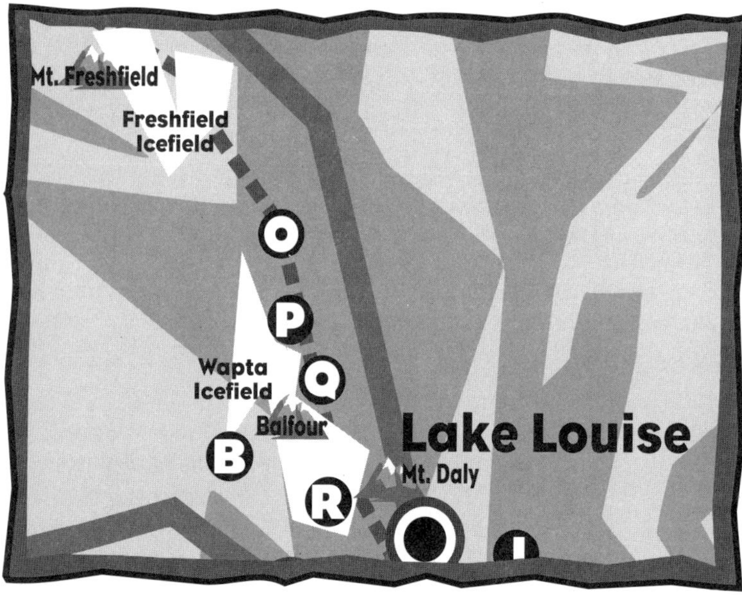

ACC Huts

O Peter & Catharine Whyte (Peyto)
P Bow
Q Balfour
R Scott Duncan

Peter & Catharine Whyte (Peyto) Hut

The Wapta Icefields

The Wapta Icefields is one of the most accessible in the Rockies, and with the four ACC huts on it, is the most user-friendly icefield in the range. The traverse of the Wapta-Waputik Icefields has a good claim to being Canada's "Haute Route," and is the best place in the area for hut-to-hut travel. Ski mountaineering on the icefields is excellent.

Travel

Each of the huts is a good base for local objectives. In addition there are three major options for travel between the huts across the icefields. The most popular is to traverse the Wapta-Waputik from north to south, spending the first night at the Whyte (Peyto) Hut and the last at the Scott Duncan Hut (it is also possible to do shorter portions of this trip). The reverse trip is less popular, but is also regularly done. The third traverse of the icefields, the "Yoho Traverse," goes from Bow Lake to the Little Yoho Valley over the des Poilus Glacier.

Traversing the Wapta in the summer or winter requires knowledge of glacier travel, crevasse rescue and white-out navigation. Travel on these icefields is a committing and hazardous affair. We recommend that you contact the Banff Park Wardens in Lake Louise to get information on current conditions before beginning any trip onto the Wapta.

The Huts

The four huts are spread north to south along the Wapta and Waputik Icefields and include one class A hut (the Bow Hut) and three Class B huts (Whyte, Balfour and Scott Duncan Huts). For the "Yoho Traverse," also see the Stanley Mitchell Hut in the Lake Louise area huts description.

References

Essential guides for travelling on the Wapta include the ***Touring the Wapta Icefields*** compilation map by Murray Toft, and either of ***Ski Trails in the Canadian Rockies*** or ***Summits and Icefields,*** both by Chic Scott. These references are indispensable for navigation on the Icefields, and most of the route descriptions between the huts (particularly in winter) assume that you can refer to them directly.

The Peter and Catharine Whyte (Peyto) Hut

HISTORY

The evolution of this facility (commonly called the Peyto Hut, but correctly referred to as the Peter and Catharine Whyte Hut, or simply the Whyte Hut) mirrors the development of other huts on the Wapta, especially the Balfour Hut. The first structure built on this site was a fiberglass igloo; the next consisted of surplus plastic bubble huts from Parks Canada; and finally, the present insulated corrugated metal structure. Unlike the Balfour Hut, the Whyte Hut has always been in the same location.

While on a Calgary Ski Club trip in 1967, Peter Fuhrmann inspired Catharine Whyte to fund the construction of the first hut on this location. The ACC got permission from the Parks to construct the hut, and then turned it over to Parks to operate upon completion. It was a 12-man fiberglass igloo identical to the first Balfour Hut, and was named the Peter Whyte Hut after Catharine's husband who had passed away in 1966. Bands of wolverines roving in search of booty pillaged the place, and thus the first Whyte Hut fell victim to the same problem as beset the original Balfour igloo.

The igloo was replaced in 1970 by two Parks Canada surplus back-country fiberglass bubbles. The bubbles were wolverine-proof, but presented their own problems: extensive condensation on the interior and a white exterior which made them difficult to see in the snow. These structures remained as the Whyte Hut for 13 years before they were removed and replaced by the present hut.

The present hut was built in 1983 by the Alpine Club, with another large donation from the Whyte Family and volunteer labour supplied primarily by the Banff (now Rocky Mountain) Section of the ACC. The responsibility for operating the hut was turned over to the Alpine Club in 1989 along with the Balfour and Bow Huts.

LOCATION

General Location

The Whyte Hut is the most northern of the four huts on the Wapta Icefield. It sits on an elevated moraine at the base of Mt. Thompson.

Map References

The hut and the approach from the highway are on map 82N/10 (Blaeberry River). You will also need 82N/9 (Hector Lake) if you plan to go anywhere on the Wapta. The other option is the ***Touring the Wapta Icefields*** map by Murray Toft.

Grid Reference

The hut is located at 314237 on 82N/10 (Blaeberry River) and the Toft map.

Altitude

The hut sits at 8,200 ft. (2,500m).

SUMMER ACCESS

Peyto Glacier Access

Net Elevation Gain

From the lake the trail rises 2,200 ft. to the hut. If you are using this route as a descent from the hut, remember that there are 1,000 ft. of elevation gain from the lake back up to the parking lot.

Time

This approach should take five to six hours in good conditions.

Approach

Five kilometres north of the turn-off for the Num-ti-jah Lodge on Highway 93 is another turn-off which leads to a large parking lot and tourist viewpoint overlooking spectacular Peyto Lake. A steep trail leads down the hillside toward the lake from the end of the tourist trails. At the bottom of the hill, the trail follows the south end of the lake and the inlet streams until it reaches a bridge to the south side of the main creek (approximate grid reference 327286). Cross the bridge and soon begin climbing to reach the crest of a moraine high on the north side of the valley. Ascend the moraine and then climb another 100m until you can traverse across to the Peyto Glacier.

Proceed up the glacier in a southwest direction, onto the Wapta Icefield itself, staying to the right of the crevasses. Once you have passed the crevasses, circle back to the left and head east toward the Whyte Hut on the elevated moraine below the northwest ridge of Mt. Thompson.

Note: It is also possible to access the Whyte Hut in summer across the Wapta Icefield from the Bow Hut. The route is over the same terrain described for winter access. ***Glacier travel and crevasse rescue experience as well as proper equipment are essential.***

WINTER ACCESS

A summary of the winter access routes to the Whyte Hut is given below. This information describes the character and (difficulty) of the undertaking, but is inadequate to plan or carry out the trips themselves. Please refer to ***Ski Trails in the Canadian Rockies*** or ***Summits and Icefields*** by Chic Scott, for complete access information.

Peyto Glacier Approach

This is the most popular access route to the Whyte Hut in winter, and is the start of the north to south traverse of the Wapta.

Net Elevation Gain

From Peyto Lake to the hut is an elevation gain of 2,200 ft.

Time

Five to eight hours are required for this approach in good conditions. Expect to add to this time if you are breaking trail.

Approach

This route starts further north on Highway 93, descends to and crosses Peyto Lake itself and then follows the general line of the summer route, with a few important variations. Refer to Chic Scott's ***Ski Trails*** (pages 160-161) or ***Summits*** (pages 36-37) for a detailed description of this route.

From Bow Hut

In good conditions this is an easy trip, but in poor visibility or white-out conditions navigation can be extremely difficult.

Net Elevation Gain

From Bow Hut the route ascends 1,100 ft., and then slowly descends about 600 ft. to the Whyte Hut.

Time

Three to four hours is standard for this trip in good conditions.

Approach

From the Bow Hut the route ascends onto the Wapta icefield and travels toward the Whyte Hut 6 km to the northwest. Refer to Chic Scott's ***Ski Trails*** (page 168) or ***Summits*** (page 41) for a detailed description of this route.

From Balfour Hut

Net Elevation Gain

A climb of 1,500 ft. is required to reach the Olive-St. Nicholas Col before descending about 1,400 ft. to the Whyte Hut.

Time

In good conditions five to six hours would be a good time for this route.

Approach

The route ascends the Vulture Glacier, crosses the Olive-St. Nicholas Col to the west and continues northwest to the Whyte Hut. Refer to Chic Scott's ***Ski Trails*** (page 170) or ***Summits*** (page 42) for a detailed description of this route.

FACILITIES

The Hut and Accommodation

The Whyte Hut is similar to the Balfour Hut and the Neil Colgan Hut. It is a one-room building with bunks on one side, a long cooking counter on the other and two large tables with benches in between. The hut sleeps up to 18 people in the summer and 16 in the winter. If the hut is at capacity, storage and cooking space are at a premium, and it is important to organize gear neatly.

Heat Source

The hut has no wood-burning stove but is well insulated and can heat up comfortably with body warmth and the heat from the cooking stoves and lanterns.

Cooking

The hut has two Coleman white gas stoves as well as cooking and eating utensils for about 20 people.

Lighting

Coleman white gas lanterns are provided for light.

Water Supply

A lake 75m to the east provides drinking water. In the winter it is necessary to melt snow.

Grey Water

A grey water disposal site at the Whyte Hut is not presently designated. It is recommended that strained water be dumped into the porous rock field to disperse it. Strained food scraps from the grey water should be packed out as garbage.

Outhouses

The outhouse is located 30m to the west. The Whyte Hut outhouse is a barrel fly-out system; please refer to the instructions in the front of the book, and change the barrels when they are full. Please do not put any unnecessary garbage in the outhouse. There is also a urinal adjacent to the toilet; this is for urine only.

Garbage

Pack out all garbage including unused food. As there is no wood-burning stove, there is no opportunity to burn garbage.

OPPORTUNITIES

Mountaineering

There are some very good moderate mountaineering objectives at this end of the Wapta; they include Peyto and Trapper Peaks, Mts. Baker, Thompson and the two peaks of Rhondda. These peaks are all popular ascents in both summer and winter. For more information, refer to ***The Rocky Mountains of Canada – South.***

Backcountry Skiing

As with most of the Wapta, the best place to find good snow for making turns is on the lower slopes of the ski mountaineering peaks. Mts. Thompson, Rhondda and Baker are the best in this area. The lower slopes of Peyto Peak could offer a great run in spring conditions.

Ski Mountaineering

All of the peaks around the Whyte Hut are climbed in both summer and winter. Some ascents can be made entirely on skis, while others must be made on foot for the final section. Refer to ***Summits and Icefields*** for more information.

The Bow Hut

HISTORY

The original Bow Hut project was initiated by Peter Fuhrmann, funded by Peter and Catharine Whyte and was constructed in 1968 by members of various groups including the Calgary Ski Club and the ACC. The hut was built near Bow Glacier to facilitate ski tourers and mountaineers entering the Wapta via Bow Lake, the easiest and most natural route to the icefields. Fiberglass igloos had been established at both the Peyto Glacier and Balfour Pass in the years prior, and with the building of a deluxe 14-person facility at a location between the two, the vision of a system of huts on the Wapta/Waputik Icefields was taking shape. None of those responsible for the project, however, could have predicted the amount of use and the level of abuse that the original Bow Hut would endure.

The hut was abused from the beginning, and saw very little regular maintenance or upkeep. By the 1980's the place was a total hole. The hut was used as a flop house, the snow within several hundred feet of the hut had been contaminated by the outhouses and by indiscriminate waste disposal, and some estimates put the number of users per year at 7,000 (19 people per night in a facility which sleeps 14!). The hut which was described upon its completion as "the Ritz" had metamorphosed into the "Bow Ghetto."

By the mid-1980s it was evident that the facility required radical change. In 1989, under the direction of The Alpine Club of Canada's Huts Committee Chairman Mike Mortimer, that radical change took place. The original hut had been built on a site which was non-porous and therefore had no drainage — a problem which led to the contaminated water and snow. Plans were made for a new hut in a more environmentally sensitive location and fund-raising began. The new Bow Hut was constructed for $98,000, raised primarily through the Calgary and Edmonton sections of the Club. Design concerns in the new hut included proper waste disposal, spacious and bright common areas and sleeping rooms which were both increased in size from the original hut and separated from the common areas to facilitate use by many groups at one time. The palatial new Bow Hut was opened in the fall of 1989 to rave reviews and is presently operated by the ACC.

The hut today is a far cry from the original Balfour and Peyto fiberglass igloos which Walter Perren, Banff Chief Warden, predicted in the late 60s "will only serve the few hardy ski mountaineers who can accept the hardships of carrying and skiing with heavy loads and are willing to put up with discomfort during the night in bad weather." It's an even further cry from the abused state of the original Bow Hut.

LOCATION

General Location

The Bow Hut is situated on the east side of the Wapta Icefield, above Bow Lake and about 1 km northeast of Mt. St. Nicholas. *Note: The new Bow Hut, built in 1989 is located approximately half a kilometre southeast of the original Bow Hut site. If you haven't been to the hut in a number of years, or are referring to pre-1990 information, please check the grid reference and a map.*

Map References

The hut and the approach from the highway are on map 82N/9 (Hector Lake). You will also need 82N/10 (Blaeberry River) if you plan to go anywhere on the Wapta. The other option is the ***Touring the Wapta Icefields*** map by Murray Toft.

Grid Reference

The hut is located at 355203 on 82N/9 (Hector Lake) and the Toft map.

Altitude

The hut sits at 7,700 ft. (2,350m).

SUMMER ACCESS

Bow Lake Access

This approach is a beautiful hike in the summer months, leading from Bow Lake through canyons, over moraines and eventually to the hut itself below Mt. St. Nicholas, at the base of the Wapta Icefield.

Net elevation gain

From the parking lot at Bow Lake to the hut, the trail rises approximately 1,310 ft.

Time

Allow at least four hours for this approach.

Parking

Parking is either at the lot immediately beside the highway, or in the spaces provided near the large public toilet 100m further. Do not park in the private parking lot beside Num-ti-jah Lodge.

Approach

From the parking area walk past the lodge to the trailhead leading around the north shore of Bow Lake. At the end of the lake cross the old stream bed on a well-defined trail marked with large rock piles, to a trail which climbs steeply above the right flank of the canyon. Follow the trail up the initial steps to the first possible junction to the left. The left trail leads immediately to a very large boulder which allows passage to the east side of the creek (there is one awkward climbing step to get onto the boulder). The trail continues from here above the east side of the canyon, before dropping down to the stream bed again. Back in the stream bed, remain on the left (east) side of the river, and follow it along the left flank of the canyon through more forested terrain which eventually deposits you in a wide moraine filled basin. From here follow faint trails with cairns (many to choose from) in the general direction of the headwall. It is possible to see the hut from this trail, high above the headwall to the right. Cross the creek at the last minute and follow good trails to the right of the creek and up the slope. The hut is several hundred metres beyond the top of the slope, just to the right of the creek.

The large boulder over the creek

Note: the Bow Hut can also be accessed in the summer across the Wapta Icefield from either the Peyto or the Balfour Huts. The routes follow the same terrain described for winter access. ***Glacier travel and crevasse rescue experience as well as proper equipment are essential.***

WINTER ACCESS

A summary of the winter access routes to the Bow Hut is given below. This information describes the character and difficulty of the undertaking, but is inadequate to plan or carry out the trips themselves. Please refer to ***Ski Trails in the Canadian Rockies,*** or ***Summits and Icefields*** by Chic Scott for complete access information.

Bow Lake Approach

This is the most popular route to the Bow Hut and the Wapta Icefields. It is not a long day of skiing, it is relatively safe (some avalanche hazard) and does not involve crossing any glaciers. Check with the Banff Park Wardens in Lake Louise about avalanche conditions prior to using this route. Please note that it is important to respect the parking at the Num-ti-Jah Lodge in the winter as well as in the summer.

Net Elevation Gain

From the parking lot to the hut is a gain of approximately 1,310 ft.

Time

Allow four to six hours for the approach in good conditions. Expect to add considerably to this time if you are breaking trail.

Approach

This route follows the general line of the summer route, with a few important variations. Refer to Chic Scott's ***Ski Trails*** (pages 162-163) or ***Summits*** (pages 38-39) for a detailed description of this route.

From Peyto Hut

In good conditions this is an easy trip, perfect if you are planning on a relaxed day of touring, or plan on bagging a peak the same day that you make the crossing. Navigation can be extremely difficult in poor visibility or white-out conditions.

Net elevation gain

There is a net loss in elevation as the route gains 600 ft. before dropping down 1,100 ft. to the Bow Hut.

Time

In good conditions, three to four hours should be plenty for this trip. If there are route-finding hassles (such as poor visibility or white-out conditions) or if you are breaking a deep trail, three to four hours will not be enough.

Approach

The route heads southwest from the Peyto Hut, and descends the slopes northeast of Mt. St. Nicholas to the Bow Hut. Refer to Chic Scott's ***Ski Trails*** (page 168) or ***Summits*** (page 41) for a detailed description of this route.

From Balfour Hut

Net Elevation Gain

From the Balfour Hut you have to climb 1,500 ft. to reach the Olive-St. Nicholas Col, and then it's a good ski run most of the way down the hill (1,800 ft.) to the Bow Hut.

Time

Expect to take three to four hours in good conditions.

Approach

From the Balfour Hut, the route ascends the Vulture Glacier until it is possible to cross the St. Nicholas-Olive Col to the west; then it descends around the west side of St. Nicholas Peak to the Bow Hut. Refer to Chic Scott's ***Ski Trails*** (page 169) or ***Summits*** (page 42) for a detailed description of this route.

FACILITIES

The Hut and Accommodation

The hut is really two buildings: a kitchen/common area and separate sleeping quarters connected by a fire-proof vestibule. The kitchen area is equipped with a wood-burning stove, three large eating tables, and tons of counter space. It is spacious and bright, and being completely separate from the sleeping area, allows a number of different groups to use the hut at one time. The sleeping quarters, which are unheated, consist of three large rooms with bunks, each accommodating 10 people.

Heat Source

There is a wood-burning stove in the kitchen area. The wood supply is under the kitchen window, on the east side of the hut. Please restock the supply inside the hut with cut and split wood.

Cooking

The hut is well equipped with three Coleman white gas stoves, dishes for 30 people, and adequate cooking pots and utensils for large and small groups.

Lighting

Coleman white gas lanterns light the hut.

Tools

There are axes and saws for cutting firewood stored in the fireproof vestibule between the accommodation and common areas, as well as miscellaneous tools.

Water Supply

A glacial stream 50m south of the hut provides water in the summer months. In the winter, water is from snow melt.

Grey Water

There is a graded gravel bed with 15 input pipes 20m east of the hut for grey water disposal.

Outhouses

The outhouses are located just outside the west door of the vestibule. The Bow outhouse is a barrel fly-out system, as are all outhouses on the Wapta Icefields. Do not dispose of any unnecessary waste in the barrels.

Garbage

Burn all paper garbage and food scraps and pack out all garbage which is not burnable, including unused food and empty fuel bottles.

OPPORTUNITIES

Mountaineering

The area around the Bow Hut and the Wapta Icefields is excellent for moderate mountaineering in both summer and winter, and the Bow Hut is the best located and best equipped of the huts for use as a base. The peaks in the immediate vicinity of the Bow Hut include St. Nicholas Peak, Mt. Olive and Mt. Gordon. To the north, Mt. Thompson and Mt. Rhondda can be accessed from either the Bow or the Peyto Huts. Information on these routes can be found in ***The Rocky Mountains of Canada – South.***

Backcountry Skiing

The slope on the toe of the glacier above the hut provides an excellent ski slope, giving almost 1,100 ft. of vertical descent to the hut; however, there are a number of barely hidden crevasses here which have claimed several lives over the years. The slopes on the mountains around the hut also provide excellent skiing terrain, but now you are into ski mountaineering terrain.

Ski Mountaineering

The major peaks around Bow Hut can all be climbed in winter, and many of them largely on skis. The most popular ascents from the hut include St. Nicholas Peak, Mts. Gordon and Olive, and for a longer day, Mt Collie. Not all of these peaks are completely accessible on skis; crampons and ice axes are required for some. Refer to Chic Scott's ***Summits and Icefields*** for more details.

The Balfour Hut

HISTORY

The Balfour Hut has seen significant changes over the years — changes in location and jurisdiction and changes in operators, as well as in the style and facilities of the hut itself.

Conceived by guide Peter Fuhrmann, paid for by Vici and Lucho Mondolfo and constructed by the Calgary Ski Club and the Alpine Club of Canada, the original fiberglass igloo at Balfour Pass was the first hut on the Wapta Icefields. During the igloo's life from October of 1965 to the summer of 1971 it withstood many storms, was totally dismantled and reconstructed with Swiss Army knives, and crashed into a moraine while being airlifted whole to a new location on the Yoho side of Balfour Pass. Marauding bands of wolverines eventually looted and plundered the hut and reduced it to worthless stench-filled scrap fiberglass, effectively ending its useful existence.

The second-generation Balfour Hut was constructed of cedar PanAbode logs rather than fiberglass and was located at a new site on the south side of Mt. Olive to the west of the Continental Divide in Kootenay National Park. The hut serviced ski tourers in this location for almost 18 years, but was eventually replaced with the existing structure at another new site at the toe of the Vulture Glacier, back in its original home of Banff National Park.

Today, with a durable metal exterior, the Balfour Hut could be compared to the brick house in the story of the three little pigs; fiberglass and cedar would be straw and sticks against the vicious storms which howl over the Wapta. The hut was built in the fall of 1989, using a reliable design which had tested successfully with the Whyte Hut and the Neil Colgan Hut, two other locations known for severe storms and harsh conditions. The hut has been operated by the Alpine Club of Canada since its reconstruction in Banff in 1989.

LOCATION

General Location

The Balfour Hut is found on low, rocky hills at the toe of the Vulture Glacier. It is east of Balfour Pass and the Continental divide, just inside the Banff Park boundary. *Note: The new Balfour Hut was built in 1989, and the location was changed in this process. If you haven't been to the hut in a number of years, or are referring to pre-1990 information, please check the grid reference and a map.*

Map References

The hut is on map 82N/9 (Hector Lake). You will also need 82N/10 (Blaeberry River) to travel north to the Bow and Peyto Huts. The other option is the ***Touring the Wapta Icefields*** map by Murray Toft.

Grid Reference

The hut is located at 375157 on 82N/9 (Hector Lake) and the Toft map.

Altitude

The hut sits at 8,100 ft. (2,470m).

ACCESS

Access to the Balfour Hut in both summer and winter is via the same routes. You can either cross the Wapta Icefield from the Bow or Whyte (Peyto) Huts, or access the hut from the south across the Waputik Icefield from the Scott Duncan

Hut. Both of these routes travel over the same terrain in the winter and in the summer, with route adjustments for crevasses, avalanche hazards, and so on. ***Glacier travel and crevasse rescue experience as well as proper equipment are essential.***

For winter access, a summary of these routes is given below. This information describes the character and difficulty of the undertaking, but is inadequate to plan or carry out the trips themselves. Please refer to ***Ski Trails in the Canadian Rockies***, or ***Summits and Icefields*** by Chic Scott for complete access information.

From the North

As well as the following in winter

This is the most popular access route to the hut in both winter and summer. Under good conditions Balfour can be reached easily in a day from either the Bow Hut or from the Whyte Hut further north.

Net Elevation Gain

From the Whyte Hut you will gain 1,400 ft. to the Olive-St. Nicholas Col, before descending 1,500 ft. to the Balfour Hut.

Time

In the summer, six to eight hours are required for the whole trip from the Whyte Hut and about three to five if you are starting from the Bow Hut. In winter, five to six hours traveling from the Whyte Hut should be sufficient in good conditions.

Approach

From the Whyte Hut the route ascends the Wapta Icefield to the southeast, and passes St. Nicholas Peak on its west side. From the Bow Hut, the route ascends onto the glacier in a northwesterly direction and circles back to the south around the west side of St. Nicholas, where the two approaches from the north join and follow the same route. From the west side of St. Nicholas, the route ascends to the St. Nicholas-Olive Col, crossing onto its east side before descending the Vulture Glacier to the hut at its terminus. Refer to Chic Scott's ***Ski Trails*** (pages 169-170) or ***Summits*** (page 42) for a detailed description of these routes in winter.

From the South

The Scott Duncan Hut is located some 10 km south of the Balfour Hut. It is not common to access the icefields from the south, and the route between the two huts is usually done from north to south (from Balfour to Scott Duncan), but the trip is occasionally made in the other direction. This section of the Wapta/Waputik is the one of the most wild and demanding from both a terrain and a navigation standpoint. It is recommended that this trip (or the reverse trip) only be undertaken in favorable conditions with stable snow and good visibility.

Net Elevation Gain

As well as the following in winter

From Scott Duncan the route ascends about 800 ft. to the Balfour High Col, and then descends 1,700 ft. to the Balfour Hut.

Time

You can travel this route in four to five hours in the winter, but expect to take a couple of hours longer in the summer.

Approach

From the Scott Duncan Hut, proceed across the Waputik Icefield to the northwest and up to the Balfour High Col. From the col, continue for a kilometre or so in a northwesterly direction parallel to the ridge line of Balfour (potential danger from icefall from above) until the terrain steepens and it is possible to turn right and pass a large cliff via a steep narrow ramp on its left. From the bottom of the ramp, proceed north to the toe of the Vulture Glacier and the Balfour Hut. Refer to Chic Scott's ***Ski Trails*** (page 168) or ***Summits*** (page 41) for a detailed description of this route in winter.

FACILITIES

The Hut and Accommodation

Balfour is a one-room hut for 18 people (16 in the winter) in the same style as the Whyte Hut and the Neil Colgan Hut in the Valley of the Ten Peaks. There is a long two-tiered bunk on one wall, and a long cooking counter on the other, and several tables with benches. The greatest concern when there are large groups staying in the hut is the organization of everyone's gear, since space storage is limited.

Heat Source

The hut is well insulated and stays warm in the winter with body heat, the lanterns on and a bunch of cooking happening, but there is no wood-burning stove.

Cooking

The hut has two Coleman white gas stoves, as well as cooking and eating utensils for about 20 people.

Lighting

Coleman white gas lanterns provide light in the hut.

Water Supply

There is a glacial stream 150m to the north which is accessible in the summer; otherwise, water is from snow melt.

Grey Water

There is a grey water disposal pipe sticking out of the ground beside the outhouse.

Outhouses

The outhouse is located just outside the front door of the hut. The Balfour outhouse is a barrel fly-out system; please refer to the instructions in the front of the book, and change the barrels when they are full. Please do not put any unnecessary garbage in the outhouse.

Garbage

Pack out all garbage including unused food. As there is no wood-burning stove, there is no opportunity to burn garbage.

OPPORTUNITIES

Mountaineering

There are not as many mountaineering objectives accessible from the Balfour hut as from the northern huts on the Wapta. Mt. Balfour, however, is one of the most challenging peaks on the Icefield, and is a great objective in both summer and winter. The North Ridge and the Northeast Face Routes are best accessed from the Balfour Hut; the Southeast Ridge is best accessed from the Scott Duncan Hut. The ascent of Mt. Olive is also a popular outing from the Balfour Hut. For more information, refer to ***The Rocky Mountains of Canada – South.***

Backcountry Skiing

The Vulture Glacier and the slopes of Mt. Olive provide for some good skiing, and just over Balfour Pass, the Diableret Glacier to the south makes an excellent run.

Ski Mountaineering

The ascents of Mt. Olive and Mt. Balfour fall into this category in the winter. Mt. Balfour requires a good deal more climbing after you have taken your skis off, and is more challenging than most of the peaks accessible from the Wapta huts. Refer to ***Summits and Icefields*** for more information.

The Scott Duncan Hut

HISTORY

The Scott Duncan Hut was the final hut established on the Wapta Icefields. Although the Balfour and Bow Huts were upgraded with much needed new buildings in 1989, it was the Scott Duncan Hut, built in 1988, which completed the Wapta system, and firmly established the traverse of the Wapta/Waputik Icefields as Canada's Haute Route.

The hut was funded largely by the Duncan family of Calgary as a memorial to their son Scott, a gifted ski mountaineer and alpinist who died in 1985. The hut was constructed by the Rocky Mountain section of the ACC and has been operated by the Club since it was built.

The hut greatly increases the safety of ski touring on the Wapta Icefield. From here, ski tourers are able to descend conveniently from the icefields to the highway in the safer hours early in the day.

LOCATION

General Location

The Scott Duncan Hut is located on a bench just above a rock bluff on the northwest shoulder of Mt. Daly.

Map References

The hut is on map 82N/9 (Hector Lake). You will also need 82N/10 (Blaeberry River) to travel north to the Bow and Whyte Huts. The other option is the ***Touring the Wapta Icefields*** map by Murray Toft.

Grid Reference

The hut is located at 417084 on 82N/9 (Hector Lake) and the Toft map.

Altitude

The hut sits at 9,100 ft. (2,773m).

ACCESS

Access to the Scott Duncan Hut is most often from the Balfour Hut. It is possible to access the hut from the south, either up from Sherbrooke Lake or, less commonly, the Bath Glacier. These routes are more frequently used as exits from the icefields, and usually in the winter. The route from the Balfour Hut follows the same terrain in both summer and winter, with route adjustments for crevasses, avalanche hazards, and so on. ***Glacier travel and crevasse rescue experience as well as proper equipment are essential.***

For winter access, a summary of these routes is given below. This information describes the character and difficulty of the undertaking, but is inadequate to plan or carry out the trips themselves. Please refer to ***Ski Trails in the Canadian Rockies*** or ***Summits and Icefields*** by Chic Scott for complete access information.

From the Balfour Hut

This is the most common way to access the Scott Duncan in both winter and summer. The terrain between these two huts is some of the most demanding and unforgiving on the icefields and it is recommended that this trip (or the reverse trip) only be undertaken in favorable conditions with stable snow and good visibility.

Net Elevation Gain

From the Balfour Hut, the route ascends about 1,700 ft., and then loses about 800 ft. to the Scott Duncan Hut.

Time

As well as the following in winter

Five to six hours should be sufficient for this trip in the winter. In the summer expect to add a couple of hours.

Approach

From the Balfour Hut, ascend the Waputik Icefield in the general direction of the Balfour High Col, staying to the right of a large cliff band on the glacier. Approach the cliff band from its left side, before turning right and ascending a ramp along its base; turn left again at its crest and head toward the Balfour High Col. The High Col can be hazardous in both summer and winter. There are crevasses on the slope heading toward the col, and danger of icefall on the right from Mt. Balfour; don't stop for lunch in this area. The route then crosses Balfour High Col, and descends in a southeasterly direction directly toward Mt. Daly and the Scott Duncan Hut on its northwest shoulder. Refer to Chic Scott's ***Ski Trails*** (pages 169-170) or ***Summits*** (page 42) for a detailed description of this route in winter.

From the South (West Louise Lodge)

As well as the following in winter

The route around the east side of Sherbrooke Lake and following the west fork of Niles Creek to the southeast ridge of Mt. Niles is the only logical way to approach the Scott Duncan Hut from the south, and the only reasonable descent in the summer months.

Net elevation gain

The route ascends 3,900 ft. from the lodge to the hut.

Time

Six or seven hours will likely be necessary for this route. There is a lot of elevation gain, and about 11 km of travelling.

Approach

Begin at a picnic area about 400m west of West Louise (Wapta) Lodge. The route follows the trail to Sherbrooke Lake and around its east shore before following the west fork of the creek on its north side. At about grid reference 407038 the trail dies out and the route takes to the open alpine meadows, following game trails where possible, toward the southeast ridge of Mt. Niles. Follow the ridge itself until it is convenient to drop down to the snow of the Niles Glacier under the east face of Mt. Niles. It is also possible to drop down to the east immediately upon arriving at the southeast ridge of Niles, to a bench approximately 200 ft. lower. You can follow this bench to the slopes below the Niles Glacier if the conditions do not permit walking on the ridge. Follow the Niles Glacier northeast to the hut.

This route is also used to descend from the hut in the summer; follow it in reverse. Do not attempt to descend to the north fork of Niles Creek directly (the traditional Sherbrooke Lake winter route) in summer; once below treeline, the route becomes an overgrown tangle of avalanche debris where progress is extremely arduous.

DESCENTS FROM THE WAPTA

Traditional Sherbrooke Lake Descent and Schiesser/Lomas Descent

Both of these routes are used as descents from the hut and exits from the icefields in the winter. The Schiesser/Lomas route is the safer, and therefore the recommended route. Please refer to Chic Scott's ***Ski Trails*** (pages 165-166) or ***Summits*** (pages 47-48) for a detailed description of these descent routes in winter. In the summer months only the Schiesser/Lomas route is recommended as a descent.

Bath Glacier Descent

In the winter, this is a good alternative to the Sherbrooke Lake exits. From the Scott Duncan Hut, this route ascends to a pass on the northeast side of Mt. Daly and traverses the Bath Glacier in its entirety, before dropping down to treeline on the east side of Paget Peak. This route should only be considered in the best conditions. Refer to Chic Scott's ***Ski Trails*** (page 167) or ***Summits*** (pages 47-48) for a detailed description of this route.

FACILITIES

The Hut and Accommodation

Scott Duncan is a one-room hut in the style of the Whyte, Balfour and Neil Colgan huts, but a little smaller. The hut sleeps 12 people in summer and winter, has a bunk on one side and a long counter on the other. As with the other Class B huts on the Wapta, good organization of personal gear is important when the hut is full.

Heat Source

The hut is not heated with a wood-burning stove, but is well insulated and warms up to a comfortable temperature quickly with body heat and the heat from the stoves and lanterns, even in the winter.

Cooking

The hut has two Coleman white gas stoves as well as cooking and eating utensils for 12 people.

Lighting

Coleman white gas lanterns are provided for light.

Water Supply

The water source is primarily snow melt, although in the summer small run-offs may be available.

Grey Water

There is a ground sump 5m west of the hut. In the winter it may be necessary to excavate the site.

Outhouses

The outhouse is located 15m behind the hut. The Scott Duncan outhouse is a barrel fly-out system; please refer to the instructions in the front of the book, and change the barrels when they are full. Please do not put any unnecessary garbage in the outhouse.

Garbage

All garbage must be packed out from the hut, including all unused food.

OPPORTUNITIES

Mountaineering

Mt. Balfour, the "King of the Wapta," is a worthy objective in both summer and winter. The standard route on the Southeast Ridge is best accessed from the Scott Duncan Hut. Mt. Daly is also an objective from the hut, the ascent being an easy snow climb in the winter. Refer to ***The Rocky Mountains of Canada – South***, and ***Summits and Icefields*** for further information.

Alpine Rock Climbing

This area is not exactly renowned for rock climbing, but one route worthy of mention is the East Face of Mt. Niles. The route goes at III, 5.8 R, and is reported to be of good quality, particularly in the upper pitches. There is potential for further development of the east face, as well as the north face of this peak, with similar rock routes. There is a detailed route description of the East Face Route in the 1992 edition of the ***Canadian Alpine Journal,*** (pages 73-74).

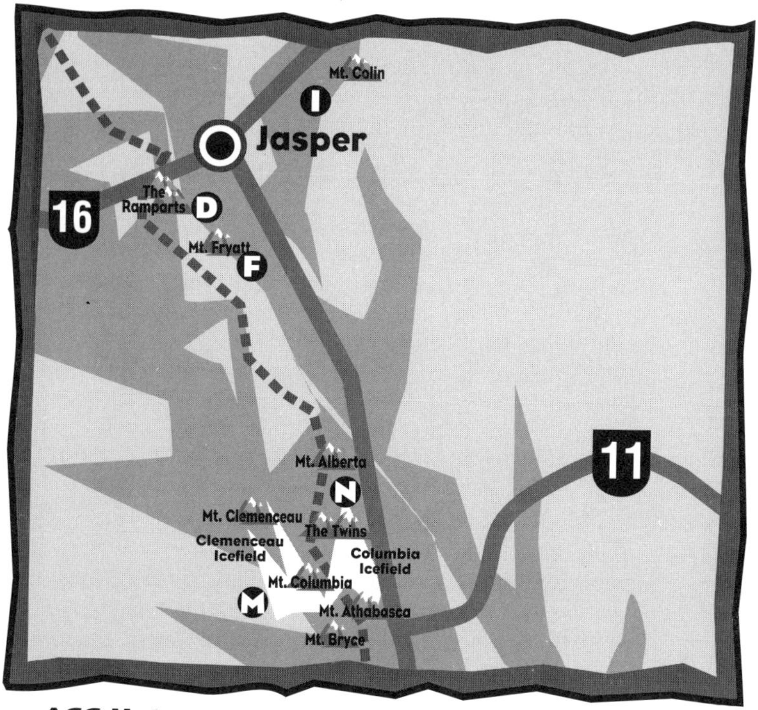

ACC Huts

D Wates-Gibson
F Sydney Vallance (Fryatt)
I Mt. Colin Centennial
M Lawrence Grassi
N Lloyd MacKay (Mt. Alberta)

Jasper Area Huts

There are five Alpine Club of Canada backcountry huts in Jasper National Park and the surrounding area. These huts are used less than the huts around the Lake Louise Area, but are also generally more difficult to access. The two class A huts (the Wates-Gibson Memorial Hut and the Fryatt Hut) are used in both summer and winter, while the three Class B huts are used primarily in the summer. The huts are all excellent bases for mountaineering, and the Wates-Gibson, Fryatt and Lawrence Grassi Huts make excellent ski huts as well.

The Wates-Gibson Memorial Hut

HISTORY

The present Wates-Gibson Memorial Hut is the third ACC structure on the third different plot of land to serve skiers and climbers in the Eremite-Tonquin Valley. The original Memorial Hut was on Penstock Creek some 500m north of the present hut site. It was built in 1930 and lasted 17 years before the foundation gave way and a better location was sought. The Wates-Memorial Hut remained for the next 12 years on the north shore of Outpost Lake. Unfortunately the location was too close to the shore of the lake for expansion, and in 1959 when the ACC applied to Jasper National Park for a permit to enlarge the hut, it was turned down. The completely new Wates-Gibson Memorial Hut was built on the present site in 1959 after the idea of moving the existing hut and then renovating it was rejected.

The Edmonton section of the ACC initiated the idea for a climbing and skiing hut in the Jasper area in 1927, but found they could not finance it alone. They approached the National Club to assist with the financing, specifically from two funds: the Soldier's Memorial Fund, set up in remembrance of Canadians who gave their lives in the Great War, and the Slark-Rutishauser Fund, established in the memory of the first ascentionists of Redoubt Peak in the Ramparts. Redoubt, named in concurrence with the rampart-fortress-barricade motif of the area, refers to a protected place of refuge; ironically, Slark and Rutishauser apparently had an accident while descending and they were never seen again. The first hut, built on the north shore of Penstock Creek in 1930 with money from these funds, was simply named the Memorial Hut.

Cyril G. Wates was a well known climber and Club member to the time of his death in 1946. Among other climbing accomplishments, Wates participated in the first ascent of Mt. Geikie, the highest mountain in the Ramparts. Wates was active in the administration of the Club and a driving force behind the construction of the original Memorial Hut, and served as Club President from 1938 to 1940. The second hut in the area, the Wates-Memorial Hut, was a fitting tribute to a true lover of the Rampart area and a man for whom "the mountains weaved a thread of worship... a thread of peace."

The Ramparts in summer.

Upon the building of the third hut in the area, the name of Rex Gibson was added to its title. Gibson was the president of the Club from 1955 to 1957, when he died in a climbing accident after being elected to a second term. Gibson also had a strong affinity for the Tonquin Valley and the Ramparts in particular, where he did much of his earlier climbing with Cyril Wates.

LOCATION

General Location

The hut is located on the north shore of Outpost Lake in the Eremite/Tonquin Valley, Jasper National Park, Alberta.

Map References

The hut and the climbing and skiing in the area are found on 83D/9 (Amethyst Lakes). The approach to the hut via the Astoria River is also found on this map; however, the approach over Maccarib Pass additionally requires 83D/16 (Jasper). Note that 83D/16 (Jasper) is a metric map, while 83D/9 (Amethyst Lakes) is imperial. Metric maps have contour lines at 20-metre intervals up to 2,000m and at 40-metre intervals above 2,000m. Translating contour lines between metric and imperial maps can be difficult.

Grid Reference

The hut is at 152353 on 83D/9.

Altitude

The hut is at 6,235 ft. (1,900m).

SUMMER ACCESS

Access to the hut in the summer months is either over Maccarib Pass, or up the Astoria River from the Edith Cavell Hostel. The Astoria River route is the fastest way into the area, while the Maccarib Pass route is without a doubt more scenic. Both routes are well defined, but can be very muddy early in the season and are subject to occasional closures due to bears.

Astoria River Access

Net Elevation Gain

From the Edith Cavell Hostel parking lot the trail loses about 250 ft. to the first crossing of the Astoria, and then gains about 800 ft. up river to the hut. Taking into account that this hike is about 19 km long, and the only real section of uphill is just before the hut, it could be considered pretty much flat.

Time

Five to six hours is standard for this hike, although fast parties can get there in under four, pushing it.

Approach

Approximately 8 km south of the Jasper Townsite on Highway 93 is a junction with Highway 93A. This junction is well signed on Highway 93 from both directions. Follow Highway 93A south for 5.5 km to a right turn on the Edith Cavell Road. Drive the Edith Cavell Road for about 12 km to a parking area on the right side of the road by a trail sign indicating the route to the Tonquin Valley.

From the road the trail drops down to a bridge over a small creek and an immediate trail junction. Follow the trail to the right which contours along the northwest slopes of Mt. Edith Cavell and descends to the Astoria River in about 5 km. The trail crosses to the north side of the Astoria and follows the north bank for approximately another 3.5 km to a fence and the remains of the Oldhorn Wardens Cabin. The Amethyst Lakes trail continues on along the north side of the river, but this is where you want to get off, taking a small log bridge across the Astoria back to the south bank. The trail to Chrome Lake and Outpost Lake is not as wide or as well maintained as the Astoria River trail from the parking lot to the log bridge, and can be very muddy and washed out in places. The trail crosses streams, washed out hill sides, a boulder field and swampy meadows before crossing to the north side of the river again at Chrome Lake. The trail circles around the north side of Chrome Lake, follows Penstock Creek up a hill and turns south to the hut on the north shore of Outpost Lake. The final section of trail, gaining the last couple of hundred feet to the hut, is deeply rutted from the horse traffic which still uses this route, and can be very muddy in wet conditions.

Maccarib Pass Trail

Net Elevation Gain

From the parking lot on the Marmot Basin Road, the trail gains 2,400 ft. to the crest of Maccarib Pass, loses about 1,300 ft. to Chrome Lake and then gains a final 200 ft. to the hut.

Time

This approach is longer than the Astoria River Trail, covering about 30 km and gaining substantially more elevation. Allow a full day for this approach; seven to ten hours is standard.

Approach

As for the Astoria River approach, take Highway 93A south from Highway 93. Drive the 93A for 2.5 km to a right turn onto the access road for Marmot Basin Ski Hill. There is a parking area 6.5 km along this road on the left at Portal Creek. The trail to Maccarib Pass is signed at the trailhead.

The first 12 km of the trail, up to Maccarib Pass itself, is all uphill. The trail is well graded and rises continuously, but the elevation gain of 2,400 ft. to the pass is a pretty good grunt. The trail down the other side to Amethyst Lakes is a nice stroll, and the views of the Ramparts when you arrive at Amethyst Lakes are stunning. At a trail junction near the north end of Amethyst Lakes, turn left and follow signs to Amethyst Campground and Clitheroe Campground beyond. Just before the Clitheroe Campground is a trail junction with Surprise Point Campground signed to the right. Take the trail to Surprise Point and follow it south to Chrome Lake. From Chrome Lake, the trail follows the same route as the Astoria River trail, following Penstock Creek uphill to the west and the Wates-Gibson Hut on the north shore of Outpost Lake.

WINTER ACCESS

The winter access routes to the hut generally follow the same terrain as the summer trails. There are however some important differences and hut users should refer to Chic Scott's ***Ski Trails in the Canadian Rockies*** for a complete description. The descriptions below are only a summary of the routes in winter, and while the information describes the character and difficulty of the undertaking, it is inadequate to plan or carry out the trips themselves.

Astoria River Route

The route begins down at the bottom of the Edith Cavell Road, where it turns off from Highway 93A. This road is not plowed in the winter. The trip up the road to the summer trailhead is a ski trip in its own right, and a night is usually spent at the Edith Cavell Hostel.

The hostel is locked in the winter, but is available by picking up a key and leaving a deposit. The following arrangements must be made to stay at the hostel:

- Reserve your place at the Hostel by calling the Jasper Hostel at (403) 852-3215, fax (403) 852-5560. Reservations are mandatory, and they will require a Visa or Mastercard number to guarantee the booking.
- Pick up a key to the Edith Cavell Hostel at the Jasper Hostel which is located about 3 km up the Skytram road and about 0.5 km before the skytram parking area. The turnoff for the Skytram road is located south of Jasper on Highway 93, about 2 km south of the Highway 16 intersection. The Hostel is open from 8:00 am to 11:00 pm, Sunday to Thursday, and 8:00 am to 12:00 pm Friday and Saturday. You will be required to leave a refundable $50 deposit for the key and sign a risk acknowledgement and waiver form. Payment for the overnights at the Edith Cavell Hostel must be made at this time. The rates as of January 1, 1995 are $9 for members and $14 for non-members of the Hosteling Association. Membership in the ACC does not entitle users to the member rates at hostels.
- Pack out all garbage, restock all firewood and clean the hostel completely when leaving.
- Return the key to Jasper Hostel and collect your $50 deposit. The staff would very much appreciate any information on the state of the hostel and the status of the supplies.

The facilities at the hostel are similar to ACC huts, with a wood-burning stove, cook stove, lanterns, complete cooking and eating utensils and foam mattresses for 32 people. Additionally, the hostel is supplied with propane and white gas for cooking and light. Water is available across the road and down a hill to a bridge over a creek, about 300m away.

Net Elevation Gain

From the road to the Edith Cavell Hostel the route ascends about 1,750 ft. From the hostel the trail gains a net 550 ft. to the hut.

Time

This trip is rarely done in a day from the highway; at least one overnight is planned, usually at the hostel. Early in the season, with a great deal of trail breaking to do, some very strong parties have spent two nights out.

Approach

The ski trip up the road is about 12 km long, and the trip can take as little as four to five hours in good conditions, or as much as a full day if you are breaking trail in deep snow.

From the hostel, the winter route follows the same trail as the summer route until the log bridge over the Astoria River at the Oldhorn Wardens Cabin remains. From here the route stays either on the north side of the river or on the frozen river itself to Chrome Lake. From Chrome Lake the route follows the drainage of Chrome Lake to the northwest and up Penstock Creek to the north side of Outpost Lake. Complete details of the route description are found in ***Ski Trails*** (pages 206 – 210).

Maccarib Pass Trail

Net Elevation Gain

Skiing this route involves the same elevation gain as the summer trail: uphill 2,400 ft. to the pass, down 1,300 ft. to the north shore of Amethyst Lakes, and another 200 ft. of gain to the hut.

Time

"A long, hard day indeed," to quote Chic Scott's ***Ski Trails.***

Approach

Again, the route pretty much follows the summer trail, except that you cannot see the trail. The ski to Maccarib Pass is a long uphill grind, but you can make up some time down the west side of it. The route crosses Amethyst Lakes to the southeast, and then goes around Surprise Point, over Penstock Creek and to the hut on the north shore of Outpost Lake.

FACILITIES

The Hut and Accommodation

The Wates-Gibson is a very large, handsome log building with the main floor divided into a large common area and a large kitchen. The upstairs sleeps 30 people comfortably on foam mattresses on two large sleeping platforms.

Heat Source

There is a very good wood-burning stove on the main floor between the kitchen and the common room. The wood supply is kept in the woodshed to the rear of the hut. In extremely cold temperatures (-30°C or less), we cannot guarantee that you will be able to warm the hut to a comfortable level, especially if the hut has not been used for a few days. You must either be prepared with very warm clothing and sleeping bags or you should postpone your visit to another day.

Cooking

Three two-burner, white gas Coleman stoves are supplied for cooking.

Lighting

Coleman white gas lanterns are supplied for light.

Tools

Saws and axes are available, and are stored in the wood shed or in the back porch of the hut.

Water Supply

Water is taken from Outpost Lake in the summer; in the winter water can be obtained by digging through the snow and chopping a hole in the ice.

Grey Water

There is a sump located outside the back door, near the woodshed.

Outhouses

The outhouses are located 25m behind the hut, slightly down a hill.

Garbage

Burn all paper garbage and food scraps and pack out all garbage which is not burnable, including unused food and empty fuel bottles.

OPPORTUNITIES

Mountaineering

The Ramparts and the peaks around the Wates-Gibson Hut provide some of the finest climbing in the Rockies. There is a great range of difficulty, and the routes have a reputation for excellent climbing and much more solid rock than is generally found in any other area of the Rockies. Another pleasant element of climbing in the Ramparts is that you very rarely see another person on the same route, or even the same mountain as you. The climbing is primarily on rock, with some snow and ice thrown in to make things interesting. Check out the route descriptions in ***Selected Alpine Climbs in the Canadian Rockies*** and ***The Rocky Mountains of Canada – South.***

Day Hiking

Popular hikes from the hut include trips up the Eremite Valley, around Amethyst Lakes, to Moat Lake, and up to Maccarib Pass. More adventurous hikers will find interesting terrain up Campus Creek to the east or further up the Tonquin Creek to the northwest. The ever popular ***Canadian Rockies Trail Guide*** is the best source of information on the hikes.

Backcountry Skiing

Some excellent tours and runs can be found on the Fraser Glacier coming off McDonell Peak to the southwest, and the unnamed glacier at the southeast end of the Eremite Valley. The lower north slopes of Outpost Peak to the south of the hut make for an excellent, but potentially dangerous telemark run. The best source of info is Chic Scott's ***Ski Trails.***

The Sydney Vallance (Fryatt) Hut

HISTORY

The idea for this hut was born in 1968 when the Vallance family made a donation to the Alpine Club for a backcounty hut. Fryatt Valley was quickly chosen, the location of the Club's General Mountaineering Camp eight years earlier, and a site with excellent mountaineering but a very long approach. The hut was constructed in 1970 and turned over to Jasper National Park for operation. The hut was initially abused, to the extent that Parks eventually removed many of the interior facilities. In 1991 this hut, along with the Mt. Colin and the Mt. Alberta (now Lloyd MacKay) Huts, was turned over to the ACC to operate. The Club has upgraded the outhouse from pit to fly-out barrel system and installed an efficient coal-burning stove to replace one which was removed in 1991. The hut is named for Sydney R. Vallance, Q.C., ACC president from 1947 to 1950, who died in 1979.

LOCATION

General Location

The Fryatt Hut sits in a small meadow by Fryatt Creek at the top of a headwall in the upper Fryatt Valley, Jasper National Park.

Map References

The hut is on map 83C/12, as is the entire approach. Map 83C/5 may be useful for those hiking further up the valley from the hut. Note that 83C/12 is a metric map, with 20-metre contour intervals below 2,000m and 40-metre contour intervals above 2,000m.

Grid Reference

The hut sits at 403174 on map 83C/12. The cabin marked on the map at the south end of Fryatt Lake (grid reference 412188) is not the Fryatt Hut.

Altitude

The hut sits at 6,495 ft. (1,980m).

ACCESS

The only access route to the hut is up the Fryatt Valley. On the first part of the approach, however, there are two options. From the trailhead there are 11.5 km of trail which follows an old fire road parallel to the Athabasca River and the 93 Highway. It is possible to either hike this portion, or (recommended) ride it on a mountain bike. The mountain biking will cut a couple of hours off the trip in each direction, and makes for a fun ride coming back down from the campground. A third option is to cross the Athabasca where the trail and the highway are closest, thereby cutting about 7 km off the trek.

Fryatt Valley Approach

Net Elevation Gain

From the trailhead on the Geraldine Lakes Road to the hut you will gain 2,510 ft. (765m).

Time

Time for this approach will depend on your choice of transportation. From the trailhead to the Lower Fryatt Campground on mountain bike will take between one and one and a half hours. Hiking this section will be more in the neighborhood of two and a half to three hours. Hiking from the campground to the hut will be in the three and a half to five hour range. Total time could be as fast as four and a half hours if you take a bike, or five and a half hours if you hike the whole trail. Parties not trying to break records should probably expect to take most of a day.

Approach

32 km south of the Jasper Townsite is Athabasca Falls and the junction for Highway 93A. Drive the 93A for 1 km to a gravel road on the left signed Geraldine Lakes Road. Take this gravel road for 2.2 km to a small pull-off on the left and the signed trailhead for the Fryatt Creek Valley. Hike or bike the fireroad trail for 11.5 km to the Lower Fryatt Campground. This is as far as you are permitted to ride a mountain bike, and it is also as far as you would want to take one, as the trail from here begins to gain elevation more

rapidly. There are sufficient trees and food-hanging poles to lock your bike to, providing you have a chain; a small kryptonite lock won't fit around the trees.

From the campground, cross the bridge onto the east side of the creek and continue uphill for about four or five kilometres to a point where the trail crosses back to the west side of the creek on another bridge. Back on the west side of the creek, the trail becomes less distinct and harder to follow on moraine and creek beds, but is well marked with cairns. The trail passes the Brussels Campground and Fryatt Lake via the west shore before reaching the Headwall Campground and the final grunt to the hut. The headwall itself is no fun. The route now rises very abruptly, and climbs pretty much straight up a trail ranging from very good to very loose for 200 vertical metres (650 ft.). The good news is that as soon as you are done the grunt up the headwall, you can take off your pack and make a cup of tea: you have arrived. The hut is located in the first flat spot in the meadow only 100m from the top of the slope.

Athabasca River Crossing Variation

The fire road trail from the Geraldine Lakes Road parallels the highway but on the opposite side of the Athabasca for 8 or 9 km before heading north. At about the 7 km point, the road and the trail are within shouting distance across the river. If you have better access to a canoe than a mountain bike, a quick voyage across the Athabasca will save you the annoyance of seeing traffic beside you after an hour or two of travel.

Net elevation gain

This variation saves some time, but it doesn't make a bit of difference as far as elevation gain. You still have to gain the same 2,510 ft.

Time

From the point where you land to the hut will take in the neighborhood of five to six hours.

Approach

The best spot to put your boat into the water is at a turnout on 93 Highway 7.5 km east of the Athabasca Falls junction. Head as straight across the river as the current allows, stash your boat in the bushes for the return trip and hike southwest until you come across the trail. From here follow the description above. It may occur to you here (as it did to me) that it may be possible, say, early in the morning when the water is not so high, to wade the Athabasca, thereby cutting off 7 or 8 km of hiking without using a canoe. This is not a wise idea, and if you gave it a serious try you would probably end up sitting naked in the trees on the far side of the river after a desperate swim to escape the deep icy waters while your Serratus pack and North Face bag dried out in the staff quarters of a Jasper resort. This would likely ruin your whole day.

In the winter the Athabasca may freeze enough to make this crossing possible on skis. Use your judgement, with the knowledge that a dip in the water under the ice would have totally different consequences than a swim in the summer.

FACILITIES

The Hut and Accommodation

The hut sleeps 16 people (12 people in the winter months) comfortably in two bunk rooms. There is also a separate kitchen/living room with a large table, two benches and a couple of kitchen counters.

Heat Source

The hut is heated by a wood- and coal-burning stove (coal stoves are very efficient when operated properly, and a pain when they are not – please read the directions in the front of this book). The coal supply is found on the northwest side of the hut, in big plastic barrels. One of these barrels should be used to deposit cold ashes when the stove is cleaned out.

Cooking

There are two two-burner Coleman white gas stoves for cooking and sufficient cooking and eating utensils for the capacity of the hut.

Lighting

Coleman white gas lanterns are provided for light.

Water Supply

The Fryatt Creek, 50m to the east of the hut, supplies the water; in the winter it may be necessary to melt snow.

Grey Water

There is a ground sump for grey water disposal 12m northwest of the front door, on the trail to the outhouse. In the winter it may be necessary to excavate the sump.

Outhouse

The outhouse is on a barrel fly-out system. Please refer to the instructions in the front of the book, and change the barrels when they are full. Please do not put any unnecessary garbage in the outhouse. The outhouse is located 30m north of the hut.

Garbage

Burn paper garbage and food scraps in the coal stove and pack all other garbage out with you.

OPPORTUNITIES

Mountaineering

One of the big attractions in the area is Mt. Fryatt itself. Two popular routes provide challenge at different levels on this 11,000 ft. peak. Other common routes from the hut include Mt. Lowel, Mt. Olympus and the North Face of Belanger.

The historic and very difficult Mt. Brussels, and Mt. Christie, are further from the hut. They are typically accessed from closer to the highway, but can be done in a day from the hut. Information on these routes can be found in ***Selected Alpine Climbs in the Canadian Rockies*** and ***The Rocky Mountains of Canada - North.***

Ice Climbing

There is not a lot of ice in the area, but the climbs which are recorded — the Ice Palace climbs, grade 2 and 3 on the headwall waterfall below the hut — are reported to be of high quality. This seems like an excellent winter adventure. Information on these routes can be found in ***Waterfall Ice Climbs in the Canadian Rockies.***

Backcountry Skiing

The trip to the hut is an excellent winter ski tour. The terrain beyond the hut may have good ski slopes as well. Refer to ***Ski Trails in the Canadian Rockies.***

Mt. Colin Centennial Hut

HISTORY

Visible from the road as an enormous fan of southeast facing limestone, Mt. Colin has always been a popular aspiration for alpine rock climbers in the Jasper area. The erection of this hut in 1967, Canada's centennial year, went a long way in making the established lines (as well as new routes) reasonable outings rather than "someday" goals for climbers throughout the area. A climbing day on Mt. Colin can be shortened by six to eight hours by staying in the hut rather than climbing the routes from the road.

The Edmonton Section of the ACC was responsible for raising the funds and for the eventual construction of the hut. The hut was completed over a couple of weekends in June of 1967, and was dedicated and opened a week before Canada's 100th birthday. Permission to build the hut was granted by Jasper National Park on the condition that it be a public shelter administered by the Park. In 1991, the Mt. Colin Hut along with the Sydney Vallance Hut in the Fryatt Valley and the Lloyd MacKay Hut (then known as the Mt. Alberta hut) were turned over to the ACC to operate.

LOCATION

General Location

The Mount Colin Centennial Hut is located on the southwest side of Mt. Colin, approximately 13 km northeast of the Jasper townsite. The hut and the approach are within the boundaries of Jasper National Park.

Map References

The hut is located on the NW corner of map 83C/13 (Medicine Lake), but the majority of the access is found on 83D/16 (Jasper). The approach for the Overlander Trail from the north is found partially on 83E/1 (Snaring River). Note that 83D/16 (Jasper) is a metric map, while the others are imperial. Metric maps have contour lines at 20-metre intervals up to 2,000m and at 40-metre intervals above 2,000m. Translating contour lines between metric and imperial maps can be difficult.

Grid Reference

The hut is located at 333723 on 83C/13 (Medicine Lake)

Altitude

The hut sits at 6,560 ft. (2,000m).

ACCESS

Due to the modest facilities of the Mt. Colin Hut (no wood-burning stove) and the nature of the objectives near the hut (almost exclusively rock climbing) the hut is rarely used in the winter. Therefore, only summer access is described below.

Mt. Colin from the Highway

Access to the hut is up the Garrone Creek drainage and the slopes on the north side of the Garrone Creek. The drainage, however, is on the opposite side of the Athabasca River from the highway and getting to the drainage itself becomes the first order of business. There are three possible routes to Garrone Flats where the trail up the drainage begins.

Sixth Bridge Approach

This is the recommended route to the flats, as the hike (or mountain bike ride) is shorter and easier than on the Overlander Trail from the north, and no boat is required.

Time

Expect to take two and a half to four hours for the hike to the hut from Garrone Flats. Add one and a half to three hours if walking the Overlander Historic Trail (half that or less for a mountain bike ride). Boating across the Athabasca could save some time if you know what you are doing.

Net Elevation Gain

From the Sixth Bridge the trail rises 3,230 ft. (985m) to the hut.

Approach

From the Jasper townsite follow Highway 16 for 3 km to the Maligne Lake Road turnoff. Take Maligne Lake Road across the bridge and turn left, following the signs which take you 3 km in to the Sixth Bridge picnic area and the trailhead; park here. Cross the bridge and take an immediate left onto the Overlander Historic Trail which continues for 6 km to Garrone Flats. The flats are easily recognizable by the remains of the historic Moberly Buildings — remnants from pioneers and homesteaders of the late 19th and early 20th century. From the flats the Garrone Creek drainage is clearly visible to the north.

Overlander Historic Trail From the North

This trail is steeper, rockier and longer than the trail to the flats from the south, and consequently is more difficult to ride on a mountain bike.

Approach

From the Jasper townsite follow Highway 16 east for approximately 19 km to a pull-out immediately after a bridge over the Athabasca River. A small wooden ladder leading up from the parking area identifies the beginning of the trail. Follow the trail on foot or by mountain bike for approximately 8 km to Garrone Flats and the beginning of the trail up Garrone Creek.

Athabasca River crossing

If you have access to a canoe, row boat or inflatable boat, it is possible to cut some time and distance off the approach with this access to Garrone Flats.

Approach

From the Jasper townsite, follow Highway 16 east for 10.2 km past the turnoff for the Maligne Lake Road to the Jasper airstrip. Begin at the south end of the airstrip (a carry of approximately 300m is required) and float across the Athabasca. On the other side climb up through the trees to Garrone Flats. It is not possible to wade the Athabasca.

Garrone Drainage

Approach

From the north end of Garrone Flats head toward the (obvious) drainage either by a direct line over very faint trails, or by following the Overlander Trail further north to a point where it crosses the creek bed in the trees and follows it uphill to the beginning of the drainage itself. Once you reach the drainage, head up on the prominent, very steep treeless slopes which border the north side of the creek valley. It is very important to get high on these slopes early on, and not to follow the creek into the steep gorge of Garrone Creek. Follow faint trails along the crest of the slope which runs parallel to the creek drainage, contouring across gullies and scree where necessary. The trail across these gullies is not maintained and is consequently rough, broken and hard to follow. There are also small sections which are a bit exposed and would be more challenging after a lot of rain or a covering of snow. Eventually the trail descends to the creek and follows a series of cairns in the drainage itself before rising up again on a good trail on the north side to a meadow and the hut.

FACILITIES

The Hut and Accommodation

The Mt. Colin Hut is a simple one-room cedar PanAbode structure with bunks and sleeping mattresses for six people (four comfortably) and a small cooking area. The hut is also supplied with tarps and hooks to provide additional shelter outside the hut for eight to ten people. The tarps are stored in a footlocker in the hut.

Heat Source

The hut does not have a wood stove for heat, but it is small and gets fairly warm from body heat and the heat from the stove and lantern.

Cooking

There are modest cooking and eating supplies, including pots and dishes for four to six people, and a two-burner Coleman white gas stove.

Lighting

A Coleman white gas lantern is provided for light.

Tools

There is a broom and a shovel inside the hut.

Water Supply

Water comes from Garrone Creek, or from a smaller creek in front of the hut. As the creek is below treeline, all water should be treated or boiled before drinking.

Grey Water

A grey water disposal site at the Mt. Colin Hut is not presently designated. It is recommended that strained water be dumped into porous rock fields in the vicinity of the hut to disperse it. Strained food scraps from the grey water should be packed out as garbage.

Outhouse

The outhouse is located 30m east of (behind) the hut.

Garbage

As there is no wood-burning stove, all garbage must be packed out.

OPPORTUNITIES

Alpine Rock Climbing and Scrambling

The attraction of the area is without a doubt the rock climbing on Mt. Colin, where a number of very high quality, moderate grade alpine rock climbs have been established on the southwest face and on the ridges. The climbs on the face are typically grade III, and somewhere in the vicinity of 500m long; the ridge climb is a classic outing. The southwest face has the attractions of generally solid rock, sustained climbing and sunny exposure; enormous potential for new routes exists.

The southeast ridge of Mt. Hawk is also accessible from the hut and is a good scrambling outing. Information on the routes can be found in ***Selected Alpine Climbs,*** and in ***The Rocky Mountains of Canada – North.***

The Lloyd MacKay (Mt. Alberta) Hut

HISTORY

Mount Alberta

Steep and imposing on all sides, Mt. Alberta, the sixth-highest peak in the Canadian Rockies, resisted several attempts and remained unclimbed until 1925. That year, a very strong team, guided by the great Conrad Kain, was turned back by poor weather conditions. Later that year a team of Japanese climbers and Swiss guides successfully climbed to the mountain's summit, effectively ending an era of mountaineering in North America. An ice axe was left on the summit by the Japanese, spawning the rumor of a silver ice axe, a gift from the Japanese Emperor. The axe was retrieved 23 years later during the second ascent of the mountain by an American party and, although made of ordinary wood and metal, remains one of the most important symbols of the advancement of mountaineering on the continent. The Japanese Route, certainly for reasons surrounding the historical significance of the first ascent rather than the quality of the rock or the climbing, is considered a classic climb of North America, and attracts climbers from across the continent and from overseas. The axe itself, sheared off low on the shaft where it was removed from the summit ice, resided for more than 35 years in, of all places, the American Alpine Club Office in Manhattan, N.Y. before those offices were moved to Golden, Colorado, where it remains today.

The Lloyd MacKay Hut

"One could say a great deal about Lloyd's climbing successes – his early days forging bold new routes on Yamnuska, his travels and explorations in the Alps, and his pioneering new routes on the Canadian Rockies' North Faces. But, although second to no one as a climber, his great strength lay in his personality. Anyone who ever climbed a mountain with Lloyd had a good time."

Thus read the obituary for Lloyd MacKay, one of the greatest climbers of his generation, who died in 1976 at the age of 36. In his memory, his family donated funds to the Alpine Club for the construction of a high altitude shelter for mountaineers in a remote area of the Rocky Mountains.

The site chosen for the Lloyd MacKay Hut was near the Freshfield Glacier. The site was selected in 1976, but due to administrative delays with Banff Park, the hut was not built until 1984. A subsequent change in Parks philosophy, however, made preserving the Freshfield Glacier as an area without human presence a priority, and the hut was removed. At that time the ACC was very interested in developing the hut system on the Wapta Icefields and, in exchange for removing the MacKay Hut from the Freshfields, the new Balfour Hut was funded by Banff Park. It was suggested that the new Balfour Hut bear Lloyd MacKay's name, but the idea was rejected because it did not fit the family's original request for a high altitude shelter for mountaineers; the Balfour Hut is more of a skiing hut than a climbing hut. In 1993 the existing Mt. Alberta Hut, the quintessential climbing hut in the Rockies, was renamed the Lloyd MacKay Hut.

LOCATION

General Location

The hut is located on the north ridge of what is referred to as Mount Little Alberta (unnamed on map, summit at 700920), 2.5 km east of Mount Alberta in the south end of Jasper National Park.

Map Reference

The hut, the approach and the climbs are all located on 83C/6 (Sunwapta Peak). Note that the contour intervals are 20m apart below 2,000m, and are 40m apart above 2,000m.

Grid Reference

The hut is located at 702927 on 83C/6 (Sunwapta Peak).

Altitude

The hut sits at 8,900 ft. (2,720m).

ACCESS

Woolley Shoulder Access

Net Elevation Gain

From the highway to Woolley Shoulder the trail rises 1,320m (4,330 ft.), and then descends 220m (720 ft.) to the hut.

Time

Climbers moving light and fast into the hut have recorded times like three and a half and four hours. Chances are that average parties with full packs of gear will take more like five to seven hours for this hike. Fresh snow on the scree slopes up to Woolley Shoulder can slow you down.

Approach

There is a pull-out on the east side of the highway 12.5 km north of the Icefields Information Centre. Park your vehicle here; the rest is hoofing. Crossing the Sunwapta River is one of the least enjoyable parts of this journey: the river is wide, and the water is cold. Damn cold. Screaming cold. Footwear such as old runners or sandals and a pair of ski poles can make the crossing faster, and some kind of insulation such as wool or neoprene socks will save your feet from a great deal of suffering in the ice cold water.

After crossing the Sunwapta, follow a good trail close to Woolley Creek on the south side. The trail starts with a good uphill grunt, gaining you 150m or so before it levels out. The trail through this section is very well defined, but may be difficult to locate. If you find you are bushwhacking from the start, start again.

The route then follows cairns and less distinct trails for about 3 km, generally on the south side, and remains close to the creek. The trail rounds a corner to the right under the base of Mt. Cromwell (unmarked on 83C/6, summit at 733908), continues through a grassy area and heads in a northwesterly direction toward Mts. Woolley and Diadem. The trail follows the creek closely until it reaches the base of Woolley and Diadem, identifiable by the bivi walls in a flat area. At this point there is no longer much in the way of a trail of any kind; you are on your own to find the best route up to Woolley Shoulder. You want to make what amounts to a big left turn under the east face of Woolley, gain the ridge of a moraine (or whatever line looks best to you) and head toward the now visible pass of Woolley Shoulder. The scree on the way up to the shoulder is repugnant and does not resemble fun in any way. Keep to the right at the top of the scree slope for the final approach to the shoulder.

From the shoulder the hut is visible 1 km away on the end of the north ridge of Mt. Little Alberta (unnamed on 83C/6, summit at 701919), but it is the last thing that you are going to notice when you arrive here. The view from Woolley Shoulder, with North and South Twin and Mt. Alberta immediately in your face is renowned and unparalleled, and few mountaineers ever forget their first time seeing it.

To descend to the hut from the shoulder, it is necessary to cross at least a portion of the glacier which lies between. The distance to the hut is short, but it is necessary to take full glacier precautions for this crossing, and be familiar with crevasse rescue techniques. From the shoulder, either drop straight down toward the hut, or (recommended) traverse across the slope toward the south face of Mt. Woolley and contour back toward the hut.

FACILITIES

The Hut and Accommodation

The Lloyd MacKay is a very practical hut. It is not palatial on the scale of the Fairy Meadow Hut, nor is it large and functional for huge groups like the Bow or steeped in the grand tradition of the Abbot Pass Hut; it is a simple one room shed with a door, six bunks and a couple of windows. It is probably smaller than what your lawn mower lives in. However it is the Mt. Alberta area, its views and (if you are lucky) the climbing that you will come here for. The area has some of the tallest precipices on the continent south of Baffin Island, enormous peaks and a scope which is often described as "god-like." The hut is a pure example of the humblest architecture of man juxtaposed against the grandest architecture in all of nature — the hut is modest, but it resides in one of the most inspiring and awesome places in the Rockies.

Heat Source

The hut does not have a wood stove for heat, but it is small, well insulated and gets warm from body heat and the heat from the stove and lantern.

Cooking

The hut is equipped with the essentials, including a two-burner Coleman white gas stove, a small set of cooking pots and pans, and eating utensils for six people.

Lighting

A Coleman white gas lantern is provided for light.

Water Supply

Water is available from either small pro-glacial streams near the hut or from snow melt. There is snow within a few metres of the hut on the glacier leading back toward Woolley Shoulder 12 months a year.

Grey Water

There is no designated grey water site; however, the area around the hut is a porous scree field, and as the hut sees little traffic, dumping strained water into the scree adequately disperses it. Strained food scraps from the grey water should be packed out as garbage.

Outhouse

The outhouse is 10m to the south of the hut.

Garbage

All garbage including unused food must be packed out.

OPPORTUNITIES

With the exception of a couple of attempts at climbing Mt. Alberta in the winter, this hut and the Mt. Alberta area get very little use outside of June to September. The climbing in the area is generally of a very high standard and quality, with routes which are long and typically very committing. The area is not recommended for beginning to intermediate climbers or those new to the area and its terrain. If you do have an opportunity to climb in the area, however, it will likely be a highly rewarding experience, and bagging a route on Mt. Alberta is typically a highlight of a mountaineer's career.

Mountaineering

There are three major lines on Mt. Alberta itself, as well as a very good route on Mt. Woolley, which are accessible from the hut. What the area lacks in diversity and number of climbs, it certainly makes up for in quality of line, history and boldness of the undertaking. All of the routes involve snow as well as intensive rock climbing, and are serious propositions in any condition.

The routes on Mt. Alberta include the standard Japanese Route, the North Ridge Route and the spectacular North Face Route, the latter being one of the most sought after difficult routes in North America. The south face of Mt. Woolley provides some interesting climbing at a lower level of commitment, good for a shorter day from the hut.

Information on these routes can be found in ***Selected Alpine Climbs in the Canadian Rockies*** and in ***The Rocky Mountains of Canada – North.***

The Lawrence Grassi (Mt. Clemenceau) Hut

HISTORY

Lawrence Grassi, mountain guide, warden and master trail builder was one of the best known and best loved climbers in the area. As a climber and a guide he made ascents of many routes in the Bow Valley, including the first ascents of the Little Sister near Canmore and Eisenhower Tower on Castle Mountain. As a trail builder Grassi is renowned for his work on the fabulous trail system at Lake O'Hara, where he worked as a Park Warden.

In 1962, Brian Greenwood and Don Vockeroth, two of the best climbers of their generation, climbed the prominent east facing ridge of Wiwaxy Peak at Lake O'Hara. The route was named the Grassi Ridge, a tip of the hat to the man who had built the extensive trails around the mountain and who had pointed out the climbing potential on the ridge. In his home town of Canmore he has had streets, a new school and a lake named in his honor.

Lawrence Grassi died in 1980 at the age of 89. In his will he left a substantial donation for a Club project with one stipulation: it could not be used for anything that could become the property of the government. The money was used in 1981 to build the Lawrence Grassi Hut on Cummins Ridge in the Mt. Clemenceau area.

LOCATION:

General Location

The hut is located south of the Clemenceau Icefield, on the southeast end of Cummins Ridge, south-southwest of Mt. Clemenceau.

Map References

The hut itself is on 83C/4 (Clemenceau Icefield). For some of the ski touring and climbing in the area you will also need 83D/1 (Wood Arm).

Grid Reference

The hut is at 320813 on 83C/4 (Clemenceau Icefield).

Altitude

The hut is at 6,900 ft. (2,100m).

ACCESS

Helicopter Access

Because the hut has seen so little traffic in its 15-year life, it is difficult to get good estimates of the costs of flights. Canadian Helicopters in Golden are the guys you want to be flying with, particularly if you are flying on a Saturday in the winter and can use the helicopter which services skiers going in and out from the Fairy Meadow Hut. If you do hook up with one of these trips, you will save substantial air time, and therefore substantial money, but you are still going to be looking at about two to three times the price of flying into Fairy Meadow. All the information in the Fairy Meadow chapter regarding bookings, baggage and rendezvous is pertinent to a trip to the Grassi Hut. Call Canadian in Golden at (250)344-5311 for more information.

Beaver Access

Flying to the area in a fixed-wing aircraft which lands on the glacier is possible, and has the distinct advantage of being a fraction of the price of flying by helicopter. There are several disadvantages, however, not the least of which is less reliable flight times (due to weather conditions) and the 7 km trek to the hut from the landing area on the glacier. For more information call Golden Falcon Aviation in Golden at (250) 344-2534.

Overland Access

Several overland routes to the hut are possible, none of which would be easy. One route is from Fortress Lake to the north, crossing the Tusk and Cummins Glaciers. Another possibility would be to follow a logging road up the Sullivan River, gain the Tsar Glacier from the east and somehow circle around Mt. Shackleton to the north or south, mountaineering all the way. Either of these trips will take you three to four days.

FACILITIES

The Hut and Accommodation

The Grassi Hut is a heavy duty, high altitude, metal sided, Gothic arch structure with a view of some of the biggest and wildest peaks in the Rockies. The interior is a single room with a double sleeping platform for 18 people (16 in winter). There are three tables, six benches and a kitchen counter.

Heat Source

This hut is heated by an oil heater. The fuel is not supplied by the ACC, but must be flown in by the party using the hut. Use home heating fuel oil or standard diesel fuel from the pump at a gas station. In the winter the heater consumes approximately four litres of fuel per day, and in the summer, about 1.5 litres per day.

Oil Heater Instructions

Prior to lighting stove:

- Pour fuel into the reservoir barrel which is outside the hut at the southeast corner adjacent to the door. The fuel flows into the hut and to the stove through a copper pipe.
- In order to remove frost in the fuel oil line in winter, it might be necessary to use a small bottle of methylated alcohol.
- Ensure that the oil control is off, the heater is cold and all excess oil in the pot is drained by removing the threaded plug from the Tee at the bottom rear of the heater.

Lighting procedure:

- Open the shut-off valve on the reservoir barrel
- Depress reset lever on oil control valve

- Set oil control valve to "low" position on the dial
- When oil appears at the bottom of the burner, ignite a small piece of toilet paper and drop it onto the oil.
- Allow heater to burn on low position for at least five minutes before increasing the setting on the control knob.
- For best results, leave control valve at medium position for an additional five minutes before turning it to high.
- If the flame in the heater becomes extinguished, allow the heater to cool before relighting the burner.
- When heat is no longer desired, turn control valve to OFF. If the heater is not in use for any extended period, turn the shut-off valve on the main tank outside the hut.

When leaving the hut

- Drain the fuel oil line by shutting off the line at the barrel and leaving the stove lit until it burns out.

Cooking

There are three two-burner Coleman white gas stoves, and cooking and eating utensils for 18 people.

Lighting

Coleman white gas lanterns are provided for lighting.

Tools

Shovels, a pick axe and various other tools are kept in the vestibule of the hut. There are a couple of heavy duty snow shovels; however, in the winter you have to dig out the door of the hut before you can get to them - so carry at least one of your own.

Water Supply

In the summer, water is available from a flowing pool 100m north of (behind) the hut. In the winter it may be possible to chop through the ice to get to the water, or it may be necessary to melt snow.

Grey Water

In the summer, a drainage pipe connected to the kitchen sink carries grey water down the eastern slopes toward the Cummins Glacier. In the winter this pipe is disconnected, so you must carry grey water in a slop bucket to the eastern slope. You'll have to dig a snow pit to contain the waste water.

Outhouse

The outhouse is located on the edge of the escarpment directly west of the hut, with a fabulous view down Cummins Creek. It may be necessary to probe to find it in the winter.

Garbage

Take garbage out from the hut. It is not possible to burn garbage in the oil heater — this will only clog up the burner. Please keep this in mind when you plan your food for a trip to the Grassi Hut.

Final Check List

- drain fuel oil line
- bring out all garbage and leftover food
- close vents at either end of the hut
- shutter all windows
- close and latch all doors, including the outhouse

OPPORTUNITIES

Mountaineering

The distances, the mountains and the amount of glaciation all make the Clemenceau Icefields area feel like somewhere between the big peaks of the Rockies and what you would expect to find in Alaska or the St. Elias range in the Yukon. The Peaks are big (Clemenceau is the fourth highest peak in the Rockies; two others are over 11,000 ft.), the space between them is huge, and it seems like there is no land which is not covered by ice.

Of the peaks in the area, the prime desideratum is Clemenceau itself. At 12,001 ft., it is one of four peaks in the Rockies (Robson, North Twin and Columbia being the others) which exceed 12,000 ft., and of the four it is the most remote and seldom climbed — this is the big rig. The other peaks in the area which attract a lot of attention are Tusk Peak and Tsar Mountain, over 11,000 ft., as well as Shakleton, Duplicate and Pic Tordu. ***Selected Alpine Climbs*** has excellent information on these mountains, as does ***The Rocky Mountains of Canada - North.***

Backcountry Skiing and Ski Mountaineering

The area is wild, seldom visited and extremely isolated. It offers long tours on glaciers, winter ascents of enormous peaks and exploration of one of the most remote corners of the Rockies. Powder slopes can be found on the glaciers and lower slopes of the peaks in the area. The hut is also a well deserved drying out stop for groups skiing the northern portion of the Great Divide Traverse, (Jasper to Lake Louise). ***Summits and Icefields*** has a complete description of the Great Divide Traverse as well as a short section on the Clemenceau area and the skiing opportunities there.

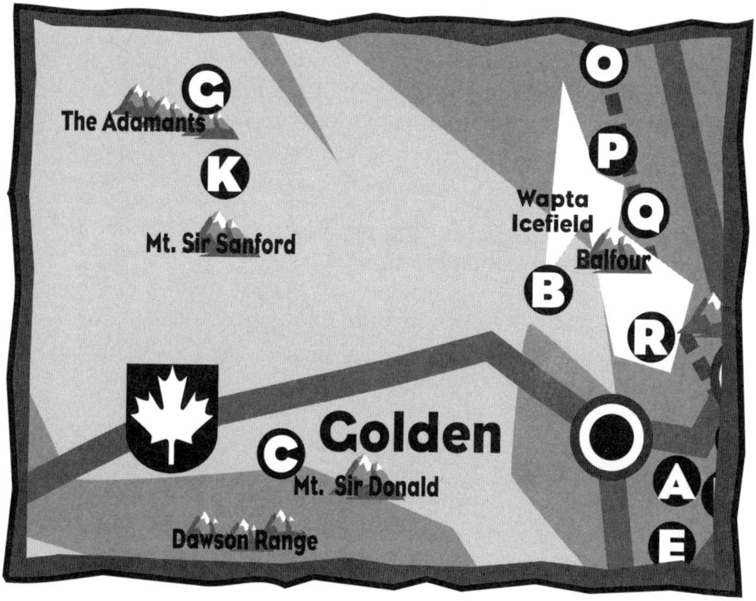

ACC Huts
C A.O. Wheeler **G** Fairy Meadow **K** Great Cairn

Huts in the Selkirks

Other than the facilities which are owned and operated by the sections, the ACC operates three huts outside of the Rocky Mountains. These huts are located in the Selkirk Mountains of B.C., on the west side of the Continental Divide. The Selkirk Mountains receive more snow, have a more stable snow pack and experience warmer temperatures than the Rocky Mountains. The rock in the Selkirks is most often granite and quartzite, a welcome change from the poorer quality limestone typically found in the Rockies. The Fairy Meadow and Great Cairn Huts are remote, in marked contrast to the Wheeler Hut, the only ACC backcountry facility which you can drive to. All three huts provide access to great rock climbing and mountaineering in the summer, and are excellent ski bases in the winter.

The A.O. Wheeler Hut

HISTORY

A.O. Wheeler

Besides being one of the founders of the Alpine Club of Canada, Arthur Oliver Wheeler is best known for his work surveying the Canadian Alps. Wheeler surveyed the Selkirk Range along the line of the railway, including Rogers Pass and the location of the hut which bears his name. He also surveyed 600 miles of the Alberta/B.C. boundary, a project for which he was the Commissioner. He was elected an honorary member of the Dominion Land Surveyors' Association, served for many years as the Canadian representative on the International Commission on Glaciers, and, among other distinctions, was an honorary member of The Alpine Club (London).

Wheeler was an active climber who attended many of the Club's camps and had a reputation for warmth, compassion and a desire to pass on his knowledge to others. He was the first President of the ACC (from 1906 to 1910), served as the Managing Director for 16 years and was editor of the Canadian Alpine Journal for 20 years. On his retirement he was named Honorary President, a position he held until his death in 1945.

It is hard to imagine an individual more dedicated to the ACC, or one more deserving of having one of the Club's premier huts named after him. Wheeler did a lot of stuff, went a lot of places and along with Howard Palmer, would be tops on my list of cool guys to spend an evening with around a campfire.

The Wheeler Hut

The idea of a climbing centre in the Rogers Pass area was not a new one when the plan for the Wheeler Hut was approved by the ACC in 1938. The Canadian Pacific Railway built the original Glacier House in 1887 as a restaurant and hotel for guests travel-ling on the line, and before the turn of the century, they were importing Swiss Guides to take the hotel guests onto the glaciers and up the mountains. For the first quarter of the 20th century until it was closed in 1925, Glacier House was the very centre of alpinism on the North American continent.

In 1938 the idea of the hut was put forward and approved and in 1945, after the war, construction began. Like Stanley Mitchell, Wheeler did not live to see the memorial which was built in his honor. He died early in 1945.

The hut has seen repeated upgrades and renovations since it officially opened in 1947, the most important of which was the Margitt Michel Annex, a major addition on the north side of the hut. The annex was built from funds donated by a deceased ACC member. The original metal bunks of the Wheeler Hut have been replaced by wooden sleeping platforms and foam mattresses, the roof has been replaced and upgraded, a propane stove has been added, new windows and fire exits installed, and a new front porch built. The hut is presently in top form.

LOCATION

General Location

The Wheeler Hut is in the Rogers Pass area of Glacier National Park, just off the Trans-Canada Highway, approximately halfway between Golden and Revelstoke, B.C. This is the only ACC backcountry facility that can be accessed by car (summer months only).

Map References

This is another hut which is inconveniently situated on the topographical maps. The hut itself is found on the bottom left corner of 82N/6 (Blaeberry); the skiing in Hermit Range and the climbing around Mt. Tupper are found on 82N/5 (Glacier); the hiking to Mt. Abbott and the climbing on Mts. Bonney and Swanzy are found on 82N/4 (Illecillewaet); and the entire Illecillewaet Glacier and the peaks of the Dawson Range are found on 82N/3 (Mt. Wheeler). Lucky for us, this is also another area that Murray Toft pieced together and compiled into one map, this one entitled ***Touring at Rogers Pass***. The Toft map is highly recommended.

Grid Reference

On both the Toft Map and 82N/6 (Blaeberry) the hut is located at 657791.

Altitude

The hut sits at approximately 4,100 ft. (1,250m).

ACCESS

Illecillewaet Campground Approach

Three and a half kilometres south of the information centre at Rogers Pass is a turn-off on the south side of the highway which is signed for the Illecillewaet Campground. The road goes straight through the campground for about 1.2 km to a "T" intersection. The hut is located immediately to the left of the intersection.

in winter

In the winter the road to the campground is not plowed, and there is a short ski to access the hut from the highway. Parking in the winter is 200m south of the Illecillewaet Campground turn-off, just south of a bridge over the Illecillewaet River. From the parking area, ski up the old road bank to the southeast from the highway until you reach the old railway grade. Turn left and follow it to the hut.

Net elevation gain

The elevation gain is insignificant, perhaps 150 ft. from the highway to the hut.

Time

Skiing to the hut from the highway should take between 15 and 20 minutes. In the summer the trip does not take any time at all; you park 100 metres from the hut.

FACILITIES

The Hut and Accommodation

Situated a quiet distance from the Trans-Canada Highway among towering hemlocks, and built with classic log cabin styling and a steeply pitched roof, the Wheeler Hut has a trunk full of charm. The interior is spacious, well laid out and functional; the upstairs sleeps 30 people (24 in the winter) very comfortably in three separate sleeping areas.

Heat Source

There are three wood stoves in the three separate rooms of the Hut. The wood shed is located 15m out the back door.

Cooking

Cooking is done primarily on a four-burner propane range. The propane tanks are stored out the back door of the hut, and can be filled up at the Petro-Can station at the summit of Rogers Pass (note: the attendants at the station will not fill propane tanks after dark). The propane supply is the responsibility of the hut user; please refill tanks which you empty. The kitchen is well equipped with complete cooking and eating utensils for 30 people.

Lighting

Coleman white gas lanterns are provided for light.

Tools

Axes, saws and other tools are usually stored just inside the rear door of the hut, or in the wood shed.

Water Supply

Water can be obtained from a black plastic line located 8m east of the woodshed (across the road). The location is marked with a pole and should be flowing year round.

Grey Water

Grey water can be poured through the sieve and funnel located in the kitchen. All food bits strained in the sieve should be burned or packed out as garbage.

Outhouse

The outhouse is a vault facility and is located 15m north, out the back door of the hut beside the woodshed. Please do not dispose of any unnecessary waste in the outhouse.

Garbage

Burn all paper garbage and food scraps and pack out all garbage which is not burnable, including unused food and empty fuel bottles. Garbage can be disposed of in the campground containers in the summer. In the winter the closest garbage disposal is at the gas station at Rogers Pass.

OPPORTUNITIES

Mountaineering

The number and variety of mountaineering opportunities in the Rogers Pass area is staggering. The fact that the Wheeler hut is situated near the highway, thereby providing same day access to peaks up and down the ranges, makes it the ideal base for climbing. On the north side of the highway, the Hermit Range provides many popular objectives on both good rock and ice, Tupper and the peaks of the Rogers massif being foremost among them. The Asulkan Group stretches to the south from the hut, beginning as popular hiking and scrambling terrain, and becoming more serious as it reaches Sapphire Col. The Parks Canada shelter at this col can be used as a base for climbing into the Bonney Group to the west (particularly the fabulous North Ridge of Mt. Swanzy) or as a stopover on the traverse of the Asulkan Ridge en route back to the Wheeler Hut. Closer to home, the peaks of the Sir Donald Group to the east give everything from desperate north faces to classic ridge climbs, the most well known of which is the deservedly popular and famous Northwest Arête of Mt. Sir Donald. There are very good reasons that, at the beginning of the century, the Rogers Pass area was the first centre of alpinism in North America, and the "Canadian Alps" were an important stop on the world tour of mountaineers. The very best source of information on the climbs in Rogers Pass is the climbing guidebook ***Columbia Mountains of Canada – Central.***

Note: Safety registration for Glacier National Park is available on the west side of the highway at the Rogers Pass Centre. Phone (250) 814-5232 for information about their hours of operation. Due to the extensive avalanche control in the winter on the highway, it is mandatory to register at the Centre and obtain a permit if you are skiing up, down or across any of the avalanche chutes which face the highway.

Backcountry Skiing

If there is one thing that the Rogers Pass area is known for in the winter, it is snow. From the enormous avalanches which devastated the original railway line and provided the impetus for the construction of the Connaught Tunnel under Mt. MacDonald, to the notorious winter blizzards which regularly shut down the Trans Canada Highway today, the snow, more than anything else, defines this area in winter. With a 10m annual snowfall, huge glaciers, deep valleys and steep mountains "the Pass" is a skier's dream, and a world class backcountry skiing destination. From the hut, you have the option of skiing on practice slopes, going for longer day tours up on the Asulkan Ridge or the Illecillewaet or touring into one of the Parks Canada facilities (Sapphire Col and Glacier Circle Huts). You can also head for the road, drive up to Connaught Creek and ski the varied terrain that it offers. There are many days of prime tours in this beautiful and historic area.

Day Hiking

When compared to the Rockies to the east, peaks in the Columbia Mountains are generally steeper with deeper valleys separating them. The result is a noticeable difference in the feel of the trails in Glacier Park compared to trails in, say, Banff. The trails are generally shorter here than in the Rockies, but with more elevation gain packed into the length of the trail. There are some shorter, easier jaunts, but the norm is stiff hikes with consistent elevation gain throughout. There are very few long, easy hikes to alpine meadows or mountain lakes, but if physical outings rewarded with stunning views is your cup of tea, then you will not be disappointed with the hiking in Glacier. Your first stop on a hiking trip to Glacier (maybe second, after getting settled in at the hut) should definitely be the Rogers Pass Centre at the top of the hill. The staff at the Centre can provide you with trail maps, recommendations for your level of fitness and experience and a dandy little hiking guide called ***Footloose in the Columbias,*** free of charge.

The Fairy Meadow Hut

HISTORY

In 1965 the Fairy Meadow Hut was constructed by the Alpine Club of Canada as a project proposed and overseen by Bill Putnam. In 1973 the first structure, which was woefully inadequate for the heavy snowfall of the area, was totally renovated and enlarged, a project once again largely funded and overseen by Putnam. Bill Putnam devoted his life to the mountains. He was the President of the American Alpine Club for years and was on their Board of Directors for decades. Putnam has also contributed heavily to Canadian mountaineering history. He spent half a lifetime exploring the Selkirks, Purcells and Rocky Mountains, and took part in writing guidebooks for the same areas (Rocky Mountains of Canada - South and North, Columbia Mountains of Canada - Central, and West and South). In addition to these, he has written several history books about the same mountains.

The hut is regularly used in the winter months for ski camps, both by the national Club as well as by various Club sections. The Club's General Mountaineering Camp, although not utilizing the hut itself, has been held in the Fairy Meadow area on three separate occasions since 1981.

The hut renovations in the summer of 1992 included complete gutting and refurbishing of the interior, new outhouses and the addition of a propane stove. The hut is presently in excellent condition.

LOCATION

General Location

The hut is located on the top of a small hill in a grassy meadow in the Northern Selkirk Mountains. It is south of the Granite Glacier and north of the Gothics Glacier in an area which is generally referred to as the Adamant Group of the Selkirk Mountains.

Map References

It is advisable to have both 82N/13 (Sullivan River) and 82N/12 (Mt. Sir Sandford) for a trip to this area. 82N/13 will suffice for the approach, but as the hut is at the very bottom of the map, 82N/12 is required for climbing, hiking and skiing in the area, travel to the Great Cairn Hut, and to put the mountains of the immediate area into perspective.

Grid Reference

The hut is located at 394352 on 82N/13 (Sullivan River). Please note that the location marked "Fairy Meadow" on the map at approximately 404365 does not correspond in any way to the location of the hut.

Altitude

The hut sits at 6,700 ft. (2,050m).

ACCESS

Swan Creek Access

Net Elevation Gain

From the final clearing on the logging road, the trail rises roughly 3,300 ft. to the hut.

Time

Times will vary greatly for this approach depending on current trail conditions. If the trail is very wet (as in the spring), expect to be slowed down considerably. Seven hours should be sufficient to get you to the hut in most conditions; four hours would be smoking with a full pack. Allow slightly longer (up to an additional hour) if your vehicle does not take you to the end of the road.

Approach Driving

Approximately 47 km west of Golden on the Trans-Canada Highway, take the turn-off to the right (north) onto a gravel road which is used to access the Fairy Meadow and Great Cairn-Ben Ferris Huts. This road is referred to by Evans Forest Products as the West Columbia Forest Service Road, or the "S" Road. The turn-off from the highway is signed for Big Lake Resort, advertising fishing and camping, and 5km along the road, the resort is on the right.

Warning: *This road drops off steeply to the lake below quite, it can be very rough and occasionally washed out, and is used by logging trucks which travel around the tight and often blind corners quite fast. While it is not essential to have a four-wheel drive vehicle for this approach, the added traction and clearance are welcome, and advised. The people at Evans Forest Products are the best source of information regarding hazards, conditions and activity on the roads in this area, and are always friendly and helpful. It is highly recommended that you contact their office in Golden, B.C. at (250)344-8800 before your trip.*

Approximately 36 km past the Big Lake Resort, the road crosses the Gold River Bridge. There is a large clearing on the left just before this bridge which is often used as a staging area for helicopter flights into the Great Cairn-Ben Ferris Hut. At approximately 60 km past the Resort (65 km from the highway) is the turn-off from the main logging road for the Fairy Meadow approach road. This turn-off is marked as km 111.5 on the road (logging road markers measure the distance from Golden, B.C.)

Once on this approach road, reset your odometer and proceed toward the stunning Adamant Mountains in the distance. The road becomes more tractionally challenging in stages from here and, depending on your vehicle, you may decide to park it somewhere along the way and continue on foot. From the turn-off follow the road for 0.8 km to an intersection and keep right (good parking here). At the second intersection at the 1.8 km mark from the turn-off, keep left and attack a steep and rocky hill, which has been done in two-wheel drive vehicles, but really tests your clearance. At the 3.7 km point there is a final intersection (keep right) and a decent parking spot. To continue past here will almost certainly require a four-wheel drive vehicle. At the end of a logging cut block at the 4.4 km mark from the main logging road, you can drive no further no matter what kind of monster truck you have, and must take to the trails on foot.

Approach Hiking

From the end of the road, walk along the border of the clearing and the forest until you find the beginning of a trail (there is often a cairn and some flagging tape here) going up a small hill and disappearing into the forest. The initial trail through the forest is easy to follow, and with the exception of occasional large deadfall, presents no serious problems. After a few kilometres, the trail drops down toward the creek and becomes swampy. Besides the obvious difficulties of keeping your feet dry and not losing the trail through this section, hikers must also be particularly wary of wet vegetation and steep drop-offs to the creek (which seems like a full-on river when you get this close to it). Take care with your footing, lest you and your pack go for a swim in the Swan Creek — at the very least this would ruin your day.

As the trail gains elevation from the creek, it dries out and becomes much easier to follow. As the forested section ends, the trail enters and weaves its way through a wide boulder field. Although this section of the trail is well marked with flagging tape and cairns, it is easy to lose your way if you are not paying close attention. Follow the flagging tape! From the boulder field, a large lateral moraine with a sharp ridge is visible on the left. The trail eventually gains this feature, and follows the crest of it up into the meadows beyond. The Fairy Meadow Hut is located on a knoll a few hundred metres beyond the start of the meadow.

WINTER ACCESS

Access to the Fairy Meadow area in the winter is almost exclusively by helicopter from Golden, B.C. With the exception of high level traverses of the Adamant Range, overland access in the winter is very uncommon, but has been done. The procedure involved alternately canoeing and dragging the canoe across broken ice on Kinbasket Lake, arduous hiking through bush and finally skiing up the summer route to the hut in a two-day effort. Even then the trip was supported by a helicopter group with food for the remainder of the trip. Flying from Golden seems to me like a much better use of time and energy.

Helicopter flights are booked with Canadian Helicopters in Golden, B.C.

Logistics:

Bookings

When making a booking with Canadian you will need to provide the following information: the number in your party, the dates you will be travelling into and out from the hut, and your hut reservation confirmation number. You must have a reservation for the hut before contacting Canadian to set up your flight. Canadian Helicopters can be reached at (250) 344-5311, Monday to Friday from 8:00 am to 5:00 pm Mountain Time. Canadian Helicopters requests that groups contact them again a few days before the travel date to confirm the numbers in the group and check on the weather.

Propane tanks

Propane tanks belonging to the ACC must be picked up at the airport in Golden and included in the baggage weight for your flights. Smaller groups (up to 10 people) may get by with one tank for a week; larger groups will require two. The tanks weigh approximately 40 lbs each when full. At the end of your stay, please include all empty propane tanks on your return flight.

Baggage

Canadian flys with a four-seat helicopter with a maximum load limit of 1,000 lbs. There are no set baggage limitations per person, but keep in mind that the maximum weight (average 250 lbs per person) includes the passenger, all baggage and skis, as well as the propane tanks. This weight restriction is based on ideal flying conditions and the load will be reduced as required to maintain safe flights if conditions deteriorate.

Communications

The only communication from the hut to the outside world is through a private FM channel installed and maintained by Evans Forest Products. The system is reliable and gives excellent coverage to the hut. Private access to this channel is available for a fee of $100 per week; however, you will only be charged this fee if you use the channel. If you have access to a personal programmable FM radio, Canadian can provide you with the frequencies. If you do not have a personal radio, you can rent one from Gencon Communications in Banff (403) 762-4396. They will program the radio for you (although you must confirm the frequencies with Canadian first), and send the radio to Golden by bus if you are not passing through Banff. In the event of an emergency it is possible to contact Evans Forest Products directly during business hours (7:00 am to 5:00 pm, Monday to Friday). The frequency is often scanned, and emergency broadcasts may be picked up by Canadian Helicopters or others during hours when Evans is closed. or safety reasons, both Canadian and the Alpine Club require that you arrange for such communications for your trip.

Helicopter rendezvous

Depending on whether Evans Forest Products has plowed the Bush Harbour Road, you may fly from Donald (on the Trans-Canada

Highway), or from the Bush Harbour staging area at kilometre 69.5 on the Bush River forest road on the east side of Kinbasket Lake. To get to the the latter, follow the Trans-Canada Highway from Golden for approximately 24 km. to the Evans Forest Products' Donald Sawmill. Turn right onto the Old Big Bend Highway which turns into the Bush River forest road. The road is marked with signs every kilometre. These markers begin with B25, and mark the road to the Bush Harbour staging area at kilometre 69.5. As long as the signs read B25 to B69 you are on the right road. If the signs read B70 or higher, you have passed the Bush Harbour. Two-wheel drive vehicles must carry chains at all times; even if you don't need them for the drive in, you may for the drive out a week later.

Costs:

Prices will vary depending upon where you fly from, the size of your party, the weight of the baggage, the flying conditions and whether you get to share costs with other outgoing and incoming guests ("dovetailing"). Contact Canadian Helicopters for the latest information and prices.

The ACC national office will provide information regarding other groups in the hut, but keep in mind that these other reservations could change or cancel, even while your group is at the hut.

FACILITIES

The Hut and Accommodation

This hut is a beautiful two-storey wooden building with sleeping rooms on the upper level and kitchen and living area on the main floor. The three rooms upstairs sleep 20 people comfortably without bunk beds. The living area has three separate built in benches and tables which are very comfortable, and a great fireplace. The kitchen boasts wonderful views, a spacious and bright ambience, a fireplace of its own and an additional large table and benches. A wood-fired sauna was added to the hut in 1995 and is a very popular meeting place after a long day of skiing or climbing. The Fairy Meadow is a singularly beautiful hut: exceptionally well maintained, functional for large or small groups, and set amid some of the most spectacular scenery imaginable. Check it out.

Heat Source

Two wood stoves provide heating for the hut, one in the living room and one in the kitchen. The wood supply is located either directly outside of the back door of the hut, where split wood is stacked, or directly in front of the hut. The logs in front of the hut are typically buried by snow in the winter and will have to be dug out. To locate the pile, excavate down to the level of the porch floor about five feet in front of the porch. The pile extends across the complete width of the porch and is about six feet wide.

Cooking

A four-burner propane range and oven provides the major cooking appliance. There is a small drain in front of the stove; please squeegie or sweep any water into it to prevent icing. As an alternate, there are two two-burner Coleman white gas stoves provided.

Propane:

In the winter months, the propane supply is renewed with each week's flight. Two 20 lb bottles are brought in by Canadian Helicopters who refill the bottles each week. In the summer months the propane is not refilled and groups not utilizing helicopter support should count on bringing their own white gas and using the Coleman stoves. The hut is set up with cooking and eating supplies for 20 or more people. There are stacks of large pots and pans to accommodate large groups and large meals, as well as baking pans and supplies for use in the propane oven.

Lighting

The kitchen area is lit by two propane lights and the remainder of the hut is lit by three Coleman white gas lanterns.

Tools

There is a good supply of shovels, axes and splitting mauls, kept in the cabinet on the front deck. As well, there are miscellaneous tools in the basement.

Water Supply

There is a creek out the back door of the hut which leads to a small waterfall 100m upstream. In the summer months a pipe running from a pool above the waterfall can be placed under water, which will provide running water in the taps in the kitchen. As your group is leaving the hut, and certainly at the end of a season, the pipe should be removed from the pool and the line drained as much as possible to prevent damage from freezing. In the winter months it is usually possible to dig down to running water at the junction of the ravine near the base of the waterfall 100m south of the hut. It is a good idea to mark the hole with wands so it can be found again after a snowfall.

Grey Water

The kitchen sinks are attached to a sump tank which is used in the summer and the winter. If, in the winter, the lines become frozen it will be necessary to dig a pit in the snow. The pit should be located off the path, and in the general direction of the outhouse. The largest particles from the grey water should be strained off before dumping it into the snow, either with the strainers in the sink, or with a sieve while dumping. The scraps can be burned in the fire.

Outhouses

The outhouse is on a fly-out barrel system; please refer to the instructions in the front of the book and change the barrels when they are full. Do not dispose of garbage in the outhouses.

In winter the snow load on the building may become quite heavy. If such is the case, please use shovels to remove the snow.

Garbage

Burn any food scraps, bones and paper waste in the woodstove. All other garbage must be packed out or flown out by your group at the end of your stay. Please bag up and remove most of the ashes from the woodstove at the end of your stay.

OPPORTUNITIES

The Adamants and Gothics are an amazing playground in both summer and winter. The climbing is often compared to the much more famous and crowded Bugaboos, and the area in winter is described in ***Summits and Icefields*** as "perhaps 'the' backcountry ski destination in Canada." Some of the elements that give the area such a great appeal to climbers and skiers — the remoteness and isolation, the sense of true adventure — make undertakings serious here, and demand competent and self-reliant parties. Do not take this area lightly; it is big country.

Alpine Rock Climbing and Mountaineering

The alpine climbing in the Adamants and Gothics areas around

the Fairy Meadow Hut, on the snow and ice, as well as on pure rock, is nothing short of superb. There are class I and II routes close to the hut for short days, long committing class IV and V pure rock routes in the 5.10 and 5.11 range and everything in between. Some routes, such as the big walls in the Austerity Cirque, require an approach day from the Fairy Meadow Hut to a bivouac below the route. The area immediately accessible from the hut has many summers worth of high quality routes on a dozen or more peaks, two of which, Adamant and Austerity, are over 11,000 ft.

Information on the climbing routes in the Fairy Meadow vicinity can be found in ***The Columbia Mountains of Canada – Central.***

Ski Touring and Ski Mountaineering

Perhaps even more than the area's superb climbing, the Fairy Meadow is known for its brilliant ski touring and ski mountaineering. The hut is central to the best terrain, and the runs range from short slopes just outside the hut door which are perfect for a ski before dinner to long tours and peaks and "experts-only chutes". The powder snow in the area is famous, and the number of ski touring possibilities will keep skiers of all abilities busy for several years.

Read the guide book ***Summits & Icefields*** by Chic Scott for excellent information on the tours, slopes and peaks in the Fairy Meadow area.

BOOKING THE FAIRY MEADOW HUT

It is not an exaggeration to say that Fairy Meadow is one of the most sought-after backcountry ski destinations in North America, and as such, booking the hut for the prime ski months can be quite an ordeal! The national office has attempted to set up a booking policy which give fair access to those making bookings. Please read the section on ACC Facility Booking Policies and Booking Popular Huts on pages 17 and 18 of this book.

About the Policies

Bookings for the hut are accepted one year in advance for ACC Sections (the trip must be open to all section members and advertised in the section newsletter), six months in advance for mem-

bers of the ACC who have ***Facilities Upgrades*** on their memberships, and 30 days in advance for non-members, or members without Facilities Upgrades. Booking the Fairy Meadow Hut for the high season is very difficult; if you do not have an ACC member in your party, it might be a good idea if someone becomes one.

High Season

The Fairy Meadow High Season runs from the first Saturday in February to the third Saturday in April. Groups making bookings for this period are required to reserve either half the hut (10 persons) or the entire hut (20 persons), and must book Saturday to Saturday time periods to maintain helicopter "dovetails". *See the rates insert sheet (p.18) for high season prices.*

Upon booking the hut, the group must pay a $200 deposit. 50% of the remainder of the balance must be paid 60 days prior to the first night of the booking. The remaining balance must be paid 14 days prior to the first night of the booking.

In the event of a cancellation, groups using the Fairy Meadow Hut must provide 60 days notice to the National Office to receive a full refund. If we receive less than 60 days notice, and do not re-sell the space, the Club will keep a cancellation/change of booking penalty. This penalty is the amount of the first night's accommodation or 50% of the total booking - whichever is greater. This policy applies to Section bookings as well.

The Great Cairn Ben Ferris Hut

HISTORY

Between 1908 and 1912 Howard Palmer traveled, climbed and extensively mapped the area around Mt. Sir Sandford, the highest mountain in the Selkirks. In 1912 he succeeded in climbing the peak, and in 1914 wrote of his adventures in one of the greatest books ever published on mountaineering in Canada: ***Mountaineering and Exploration in the Selkirks.*** The Silvertip, Haworth and Sir Sandford glaciers have all receded substantially since Palmer's expeditions; the present site of the Great Cairn Hut was under 20 to 30m of ice where the three glaciers met in Palmer's day.

In 1953, a party from the Harvard Mountaineering Club was on a climbing trip in the area and on a rainy August day built a 20-foot high cairn, known as the Great Cairn. In 1963, Bill Putnam and Ben Ferris visited the area and began plans for the construction of a climbing hut. The hut was built the following year, and finished in 1965. The Great Cairn Hut was financed by Putnam and the ACC, and was built from the stones of the Great Cairn, which was dismantled for its materials.

LOCATION

General Location

The Great Cairn-Ben Ferris Hut sits on a red bedrock bench, 4 km north-northwest of Mt. Sir Sandford in the heart of the Northern Selkirk Mountains of B.C.

Map References

The hut is on map 82N/12 (Mount Sir Sandford). The approach

from the Fairy Meadow Hut also requires 82N/13 (Sullivan River).

Grid Reference

The hut is located at approximately 392268 on 82N/12 (Mount Sir Sandford).

Altitude

The hut sits at 6,200 ft. (1,890m).

ACCESS

Access to the Great Cairn-Ben Ferris Hut is either very expensive or very difficult. The two overland approaches are the longest access routes described in this book (with the exception of the routes to the Grassi Hut), and are very serious route-finding undertakings. The other option is shelling out some big bucks and flying from Golden or the Gold River Bridge directly to the hut. As G. Gordon Liddy said "I'll break your legs or steal your girlfriend — your choice, Mister."

Overland route from Fairy Meadow

This is a big day in the mountains! The route goes over three passes, crosses two major glaciers and covers about 11 km of serious mountain terrain. The Gothics Glacier between Friendship Col and Thor Pass can be very nasty with crevasses, particularly around the south ridge of Sentinel Peak, at any time of the year. Parties making this crossing should be adept at glacier travel and crevasse rescue.

Net elevation gain

Because the Fairy Meadow Hut sits at 6,700 ft. and the Great Cairn Hut-Ben Ferris at 6,200, there is a net loss in elevation on this trip, but it is sure not going to feel like it by the end of the day. From Fairy Meadow, you will gain 2,200 ft. to Friendship Col, lose about 400 ft. onto the Gothics Glacier, gain almost 1,000 ft. to Thor Pass, lose 1,800 ft. to the Adamant Glacier and gain 500 ft. to Azimuth Notch, before the final descent of 2,100 ft. to the Great Cairn-Ben Ferris Hut. The total elevation gain for the trip is approximately 3,700 ft.

Time

Don't plan to make an attempt on Sir Sandford the same-day you make the crossing. In fact, don't plan for much of anything for the remainder of the day. This trip takes strong parties eight to ten hours in the best conditions. Fresh snow could slow you down considerably by making the trail to Friendship Col hard to follow and by covering the crevasses on the glaciers. Breaking trail through deep snow the whole distance would pretty much preclude a one day crossing. It would be astute to scope out the route from the Fairy Meadow Hut to Friendship Col ahead of time (if you do not know it already) and leave the hut early.

Approach

There is a well used trail in the direction of Friendship Col from behind (south of) the Fairy Meadow Hut. The trail is well marked with cairns, but becomes less obvious as it ascends talus slopes toward the Col, particularly with fresh snow. It is important to note that the col is incorrectly labelled on 82N/12, and should be located west of Mt. Damon at grid reference 333406. The route stays to the right (north) of a buttress and follows the crest of a moraine toward the glacier. Follow the glacier east of Gog and Magog to Friendship Col.

From Friendship Col, descend onto the expanse of the Gothics Glacier and head toward Thor Pass at grid reference 398307, keeping well south of the south ridge of Sentinel Peak to avoid large crevasses. On the other side of Thor Pass descend a steep rocky slope to the Thor Glacier (unmarked glacier on 82N/12). Talus slopes lead to the flats of the Adamant Glacier. With good visibility, Azimuth Notch is obvious from Thor Pass, with a square notch-like appearance. In poor visibility you will want to take a bearing from the pass on the notch at grid reference 385285 (Azimuth Notch is also misplaced on 82N/12). ***The Climber's Guide to the Columbia Mountains of Canada – Central*** describes a "nefarious 'swamp', which, if present, can be distinguished from above by its whiter and flatter appearance" on the Adamant Glacier. If this swamp is present, you should avoid it.

After crossing the Adamant Glacier, the notch is best approached from the east, crossing the usually tame bergschrund wherever convenient. In good visibility (and particularly if the sun is reflecting against the metal roof), you can pick out the hut from Azimuth Notch at 392268 on the red bedrock bench just south of the creek flowing from the Silvertip and Haworth Glaciers. From the notch, descend to the creek and follow it to the hut. Crossing the creek can be difficult late in the day, or after large amounts of precipitation. It is easiest to cross it close to the Silvertip Glacier itself, but this involves adding an extra kilometre or so to the trip at the end of a big day.

You could take a more direct line to the hut by wading through the fast, cold water. If this were the Sunwapta River and you had just come out from the Lloyd MacKay Hut, things would be a lot simpler — you would just stomp through the water in your mountain boots, throw them wet into the back of your truck or the trunk of your car and start thinking about where you could get some beers to wash down the nachos you were going to have for dinner. But approaching the Great Cairn Hut, the last thing you are going to want to do is dry out your boots for the next two days. So backtrack to the Silvertip, or sploosh around in the cold glacial melt — again, your choice.

Goat Glacier to Sir Sandford Pass

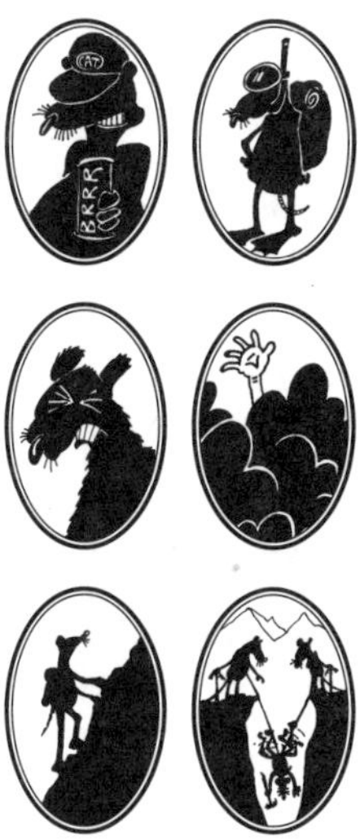

Another big day in the mountains, this trip involves four-wheeling, serious bushwhacking through serious bear country and a ten-kilometre glacier trip. This access route does, however, have the advantage of providing a one-day route to the Great Cairn Hut without flying.

Net Elevation Gain

From the end of the logging road to Sir Sandford Pass, there is an elevation gain of approximately 3,500 ft. From the pass, the route steadily descends 2,300 ft. down the glacier to the hut.

Time

This trip takes nine to ten hours in good conditions.

Approach

Follow the description for driving to the Fairy Meadow trailhead to a junction just before the Gold River Bridge (kilometre marker 87). Take this road (the "black road" in reference to the kilometre markers) to the left. The road is rougher and steeper than the red road toward the Fairy Meadow Hut and a four wheel drive vehicle, or at least one with high clearance, is recommended. Once on the black road, you will come to junctions at kilometre markers 89 and 98; stay right at both junctions, the second of which takes you onto the "gold road" which turns away from the junction of Bachelor Creek and follows the Gold River. There is one more junction at kilometre marker 108; stay to the right again, following the Gold River toward Moberly Pass as far as the road will take you. This should place you at about 360175 on 82N/12 (estimated grid reference). At the end of this road you will find some steep switchbacks which afford a view up the Gold River valley toward Moberly Pass. Park here. The pass itself is not visible from this point, and neither is the Goat Glacier. The glacier in the distance is not the Goat Glacier, but rather an unnamed glacier on 82N/12 directly west of it. Goat Glacier itself will not be visible until you round the west ridge of Citadel Mountain and begin to approach it.

Okay, here's the ugly part. From your vehicle, descend to the Gold River and follow it a short distance upstream where two equally unattractive options are possible. The first option is to begin gaining elevation immediately on the north slopes of the river. Use avalanche paths to proceed upwards wherever possible, and traverse in a northwesterly direction through slide alders toward the lowest reaches of the west ridge of Citadel. From here, scramble over easy ledges and talus toward the southernmost part of the Goat Glacier. The second possibility is to pound laboriously up the river itself. Alternate travel on one bank or the other, as seems best, in the general direction of Moberly Pass. A single, long, direct avalanche path begins west of Citadel Mountain and comes down almost to the river approximately 1 km east of Moberly Pass. This avalanche path provides access to the lower reaches of the west ridge of Citadel and the Goat Glacier beyond (the glacier is not visible from the river). From the top of the avalanche path the glacier is visible and is accessible by easy scrambling and talus.

It seems as though one access to the Goat Glacier is as good (or as bad) as the other. Both involve grunting in alders through very serious bear country. The first option does, however, have the advantage of travelling through prime raspberry, blackberry and huckleberry terrain late in the year. Following the river may be preferable if using this route as a descent from the Goat Glacier, when you are not going to be as concerned about getting your feet wet.

Ascending the Goat Glacier will likely be the most technically challenging aspect of this approach. The middle part of the glacier is steep and crevassed. A wide ramp starting on the right side of the glacier and angling up and left presents an easy passage to the final slopes to Sir Sandford Pass. Expect technical terrain on this portion of the glacier, and large crevasses for the entire trip. From the summit of the pass, proceed to the northeast down the Sir Sandford Glacier in the general direction of Ravelin Mountain. On the east side of the lower Sir Sandford Glacier there is a large lateral moraine which runs between the northwest face of the Ravelin and the northwest ridge of Vidette Peak. Cross this moraine as soon as it is convenient, and travel the remainder of the glacier on the right (east) side of it. This route provides an easy exit from the glacier onto the moraine around the north side of Ravelin Mountain. From here contour around to the west of the Ravelin until it is possible to descend on mud, rocks, slabs and moraine back to the toe of the Sir Sandford Glacier.

Looking down the ramp on the Goat Glacier

Descending towards the lateral moraine on the Sir Sandford Glacier

Looking back up the Sir Sandford Glacier from the hut

Cross the toe of the glacier to the northwest. From here there are faint trails which contour across the slope and lead to the final scramble up the red bedrock bench to the hut.

Palmer Creek

This was the original route to the Sir Sandford area by Howard Palmer and friends early in the century. Herb and Pat Kariel, in ***Alpine Huts in the Rockies, Selkirks and Purcells,*** record that the next attempt at pushing through this route was in 1976. A rough description of the route is included here for historical relevance and reverence, and because the route is apparently obvious on the map.

Net Elevation Gain

From the Gold River Bridge to the hut you will need to gain 3,700 ft. In the Palmer Creek, these will be hard won feet, every one of them.

Time

Who knows? Palmer took the better part of four summers to climb Sir Sandford by this route.

Approach

It is clear where the effort would start (the Gold River Bridge) and clear where it would ideally end (the hut), but there are very few details available about travel in Palmer Creek. From above, the bush looks mighty thick. In Palmer's words:

"If the truth be told, our introduction to the *chevaux-de-frise* of the Selkirk wilderness was about as bad as can be imagined. Stumbling through pools of water up to our knees, fording shallow streams, falling into rotten stumps, and, of course, grabbing prickly devil's club for support, we slowly forged ahead. At each halt, relief from the attacks of our tormentors could only be obtained by waving a leafy branch continuously, for head-nets cannot be worn to advantage in the thick undergrowth."

Unfortunately, not much more is known about this route, except that it would be very difficult bushwhacking. Enjoy!

Helicopter from Golden

Winter or summer, this is definitely the most civilized route to the hut. It allows you to carry fresh food, more red wine than you could carry on your own, firewood for the stove, and it puts you at the hut fresh for the following day's activities.

Net Elevation Gain

From the Gold River Bridge on the approach road, there is a 3,700 ft. elevation gain.

Time

From the Gold River Bridge the trip is five to six minutes. From Golden the trip takes 24 to 30 minutes.

Approach

You have the choice of flying directly from the helipad in Golden or from the Gold River Bridge on the road to Fairy Meadow. Flying from the bridge allows you to shuttle vehicles into position for a return hike, be it out from Fairy Meadow, down from the Goat Glacier, or (shudder) down Palmer Creek. Flying from the bridge also gives you the flexibility of flying an additional load into the hut without having to pay for a return trip to Golden to do so. This may be an issue even if you are only planning to have one flight, as maximum loads in helicopters vary with the weather conditions.

For winter flights into the Great Cairn Hut, refer to the information on Canadian Helicopters under "Winter Access" in the Fairy Meadow chapter. The staging area is the same as for that hut, and the costs are similar, although there is less chance of dovetailing your flights.

Costs

The cost to fly is going to depend on a number of different factors. Helicopter time is charged by the hour, and differs for different machines. Canadian Helicopters in Golden flies with either a four- or a three-seater, depending on availability. The greatest cost is getting the helicopter from Golden to the staging area at the Gold River Bridge (.3 to .4 of an hour); flying from the bridge to the hut is around .2 of an hour return (all helicopter time is estimated due to wind and weather conditions). Costs per person will decrease as the number of trips from the bridge increases (and the initial trip from Golden is split more ways). The maximum load per person, including gear, is 250 lbs. Determine how many people and how much gear will be going to the hut, and phone Canadian in Golden at (250) 344-5311.

FACILITIES

The Hut and Accommodation

Situated on a bench with a front row seat for the many moods of Mt. Sir Sandford, and built from stones from the area, the Great Cairn Hut-Ben Ferris is one of the most attractive huts the ACC operates, as well as one of the most spectacularly positioned. The hut sleeps six people quite comfortably, has a mouse-proof wooden food locker and a small table with four stools.

Heat Source

The hut is equipped with a wood-burning stove; however, wood is not supplied by the ACC. Firewood can either be collected as avalanche debris from the surrounding slopes in the summer or flown in.

Cooking

Man, are there dishes at this hut! Probably due to the fact that this hut is remote, many parties have assumed that they should bring in enough kitchen supplies for their group and the dishes get added to the collective inventory of the hut. At last count the hut was fully equipped for a dinner party for 18. The hut has a single two-burner white gas Coleman stove.

Lighting

There is one Coleman white gas lantern.

Tools

There is a good bow saw and a spare blade for cutting firewood, as well as various tools.

Water Supply

The creek running from the Haworth and Silvertip Glaciers passes by the hut a short distance to the west, and is easily accessed slightly upstream. There are also some deep pools of water which form in the rock around the hut, and they can be used for bathing when the weather is really warm.

Grey Water

A grey water disposal site at the Great Cairn Hut is not presently designated. It is recommended that strained water be dumped into porous rock fields in the vicinity of the hut to disperse it. Strained food scraps from the grey water should be burned in the wood stove or packed out as garbage.

Outhouse

The outhouse is located 50m to the northeast.

Garbage

Burn all paper garbage and food scraps in the wood stove. All other garbage and unused food must be packed out or flown out by your group.

OPPORTUNITIES

Mountaineering

Mt. Sir Sandford, the highest summit in the Selkirks, is without a doubt the prime attraction of the area. There are nearly a dozen routes and variations on the peak, the most worthwhile being on snow and ice. Other moderate snow and ice routes exist on Silvertip, Citadel, Cornice Peak, The Footstool, and others.

An exception to the generally poor rock climbing in the Sir Sandford area may be the rock on the northwest side of Ravelin Peak. No routes exist, but the potential seems great.

To the northwest, there are brilliant routes on the excellent granite peaks of the Adamants. The Blackfriars and Belvedere Peak are accessed best from the Great Cairn-Ben Ferris Hut. The exceptional rock routes on the south side of the Stickle, Turret Peak and Austerity are accessed from the hut, but usually involve a bivouac.

An alternative to the peaks is a crag below the snout of the Silvertip Glacier. It is undeveloped, but faces southeast, provides very fine rock and enjoys a fabulous position overlooking the hut and Mount Sir Sandford. Some limited but exceptional bouldering can also be found on this formation. Information on these mountain routes can be found in ***Columbia Mountains of Canada, Central.***

Ski Touring and Ski Mountaineering

The Great Cairn-Ben Ferris Hut is not the ski destination that its rich cousin the Fairy Meadow Hut is: the telemarking slopes are not as extensive and the facilities at the hut are more limited (no propane stove, no firewood). Rather, the Great Cairn-Ben Ferris is a remote hut with fabulous glaciers and tons of potential for exploration and touring. It is occasionally used as an overnight destination from the Fairy Meadow Hut for small groups looking for something a little bit different and a challenging backcounty travel adventure.

Section Facilities

There are three ACC backcountry facilities which are not operated by the national Club, but are owned and operated by various sections of the Club: the Tantalus Hut in the Coast Mountains, the Bon Echo Hut on Mazinaw Lake in southern Ontario and the Keene Farm in the Adirondack Mountains of New York State. These huts have different facilities and rates from the national Club's system of huts and are reserved through the section contacts provided.

The Tantalus Hut

HISTORY

The hut was built by the ACC in 1961 as a base for mountaineering in the Tantalus Range.

LOCATION

General Location

Located at the east end (outflow) of Lake Lovely Water in the Tantalus Range of the B.C. Coast Mountains approximately 64 km (40 miles) northwest of Vancouver. The hut is located in the Lake Lovely Water Wilderness Area.

Emergencies

Squamish RCMP can be reached by dialling 9-1-1 or (604) 898-9611.

Amenities

Squamish has complete facilities including gas stations, large grocery stores, cafes and bakeries.

Map References

The hut and the approach are found on 92 G/14 (Cheakamus River) and on Provincial 92 G/NW (1:100,000) Outdoor Recreation Council of BC – Map #3.

Grid Reference

The hut is located at 819146 on 92G/14 (Cheakamus River).

Altitude

The hut sits at 3,850 ft.

ACCESS

The access information given below is for the summer months and requires that you have a boat. Access to the hut in the winter is uncommon, as the terrain around the hut is not well suited to skiing and winter climbing is limited by avalanche hazard.

Net Elevation Gain

From the river crossing to the hut the trail gains about 3,850 ft. (1,170m).

Time

The approach takes between three and five hours from the river.

Approach

From Vancouver drive to Squamish on Highway 99 (54 km). Drive three to four kilometres past Squamish and take the airport exit off Highway 99 toward Cheekye. At Cheekye cross the Mamquam River Bridge and stay left immediately after crossing it. Proceed for another 2.3 km to just past the third power line tower where it is possible to make a sharp left onto a rough road. Follow this road for 1.6 km to the river. Cross the river (about 100m across) with your own canoe, or, for a reasonable fee, you can phone and book a space on a boat operated by Jay Bicknell (604) 898-3356. If you use your own boat, the best place to put it in the river is about 300m upstream from the cable car crossing. Exercise caution when crossing the river as it is swift and dangerous; life-jackets are mandatory. The trail parallels the far bank of the river before heading up a steep mountain trail to Lake Lovely Water and the hut.

Float plane access is possible from Vancouver. Helicopter access is available and can be arranged by contacting Pemberton Helicopters at (604) 898-9688 (phone) or (604) 898-9600 (fax) or Blackcomb Helicopters (604) 892-3060 (phone) or (604) 938-1706. A trip into

Lake Lovely Water is about $250 and can be split by up to four in the helicopter.

FACILITIES

The Hut and Accommodation

This hut is a two-storey wooden structure with a separated sleeping loft and foam mattresses for 30 people (24 in the winter). There is also a large kitchen/living room on the main floor.

Heat Source

There is a wood-burning stove for heat, but the wood supply is scarce. Inquire about the status of the supply when making your reservation.

Cooking

There is one large Coleman white gas stove and cooking and eating utensils for 30 people. It is important that only white gas is used in this stove.

Lighting

Coleman white gas lanterns are provided for light.

Boats

A canoe donated by the Evans family and a large rowboat are available for traversing the lake to reach the climbs which are mostly at the far end, and for fishing.

Water Supply

Drinking water is available from the creek nearby.

Grey Water

Grey water is disposed of down the sinks.

Outhouses

The outhouse is about 30m to the northwest of the cabin.

Garbage

Burn all paper garbage; all other garbage must be packed out.

OPPORTUNITIES

The area offers a variety of climbing opportunities of various grades and classic alpine routes abound on peaks such as: Tantalus

2,603 m (8,540 ft); Dione 2,590 m (8,500 ft); Alpha 2,305 m (7,562 ft); Serratus 2,326 m (7,632 ft); and many others.

The ACC also has the Red Tit Hut, a fiberglass dome shelter at the col between Dione and Serratus. Information on this shelter is available from the contact below.

Climbing in the area is covered in ***Climbing and Hiking in Southwestern B.C.*** by Bruce Fairley. The best reference for skiing in the area is ***Exploring the Coast Mountains on Skis, 2nd Edition*** by John Baldwin.

RATES AND RESERVATIONS

The Tantalus Hut and the Red Tit Hut are supervised by Ron Royston of the Vancouver Section of the ACC. Ron can be reached at work at (604) 687-2711 (preferred) or at home at (604) 921-8164 to arrange to pick up a key to the Tantalus Hut and to pay the overnight fees. Costs for the Tantalus Hut are $10 per person per night; reservations are mandatory.

The Bon Echo Hut

HISTORY

The land on which the hut is located was purchased in 1964 by Walter Robinson, David Fisher, and Wally Joyce. The original hut was expanded in the late sixties and the fireplace built to commemorate Brian Cook, an active local climber who was killed while climbing at Bon Echo in 1969. Over the years several boats have been used to service the hut and cliff face, making the Toronto Section of the Alpine Club the only section to have a long nautical history.

LOCATION

General Location

The hut is located approximately 300 km northwest of Toronto on the west side of Mazinaw Lake, a mile north of the Mazinaw Rock and Bon Echo Provincial Park.

Amenities

The town of Northbrook, 10 km the necessities of life, including food, gas and beer.

Map References

The hut is on 31C/14 (Mazinaw Lake).

Grid Reference

The hut is at 271759 and the public dock is at 257753 on 31C/14 (Mazinaw Lake).

Altitude

The hut sits at 860 ft. (260m).

ACCESS

Approach

The drive to the public dock takes approximately three hours from Toronto and approximately one and a half hours from Ottawa.

The hut can be reached by hiking overland, but this would take an entire day. Boating to the hut is much more convenient, and therefore, the hike is not described.

To reach the public dock, travel north on Highway 41, turn right onto Mazinaw Heights Road (the first right turn after passing the main gate for Bon Echo Provincial Park) and follow it to the dock. Climbers wishing to use the hut can arrange for the boat to meet them at the dock by calling the custodian ahead of time. Pick-up times are Friday at 10:30 pm and Saturday at 10:30 am. Contact the National Office for the name and phone number of the current custodian.

FACILITIES

The Hut and Accommodation

The hut is a single-room, shanty-style wooden structure with a fireplace and a kitchen equipped with propane stoves and a large dining table. There is a sauna located near the lake. The hut is not used for sleeping, but is a day hut and cook shelter for those staying at the campsites immediately adjacent to the hut. The hut accommodates up to 30 people for cooking and eating, and a custodian is normally on duty on summer weekends.

Heat Source

There is a fireplace in the building.

Cooking

The hut is equipped with propane stoves, a sink, and pots and pans, as well as a community garbage pail.

Lighting

The hut is lit with propane lamps.

Water Supply

Water can be obtained from a spring located part way along the cliff face (at the base of the route *Birthday Ridge*), from the taps at the park across the lake, or from the lake itself. Water from the lake must be boiled or treated before it is consumed.

Grey Water

Grey water is disposed of out in the trees, away from the tent sites.

Outhouses

There is an outhouse east of the hut which is reached by following a trail on the north side of the building.

Garbage

It is imperative that you pack out all of your own garbage.

OPPORTUNITIES

Rock Climbing

Rock climbing has been a tradition at Mazinaw Rock since the late 1950s. The cliff is 350 ft. high, over a mile long and is home to more than 120 routes from 5.0 to mid 5.12. While some routes start from in a boat or from hanging belays, most begin on ledges near the waterline. The climbing is totally traditional (no sport routes), in a serious and remote location. The seriousness of the setting demands that your party is fully equipped for bad weather and is self-sufficient and able to handle emergency situations and accidents.

The area of Mazinaw Rock has recently been designated as a nature reserve. The area is home to Indian rock paintings, rare lichens and ancient trees and is being used for an on-going falcon release program. The cliff will be undergoing an intensive survey in 1995 and 1996 to determine the effect of climbing on the cliff. ***Climbers are strongly encouraged to limit their impact on the cliff and the area as much as possible. Stay on trails on the cliff top, do not remove any existing vegetation and avoid rappelling from trees. No new fixed protection may be placed, and visible climbing gear left on the cliff (rappel slings, back-off slings) should be minimized. New route activity is strongly discouraged. Note that this is a "traditional" climbing area; it is essential that you respect local practices and requests in order to preserve the future of climbing at Mazinaw Rock.***

Complete information on the climbs here is found in ***A Guide to Climbing at Bon Echo*** by Stephen Adcock. The book is available at the Mountain Equipment Co-op stores in Ottawa and Toronto, as well as at Smarts Marina at the south end of the lake.

Ice Climbing

In the winter, waterfalls form at two points, offering a choice of routes at two levels. The easier line, simply known as "the Icefall," is 15 to 20m high and is in the grade 2-3 range. The second route, *Old Laughing Lady,* forms only occasionally, and when it does it is approximately 35m high, grade 5 and difficult to protect. The area is not a destination for ice climbing, but if you are in the neighborhood, it makes for an interesting diversion.

RATES AND RESERVATIONS

Contact the Toronto Section of the ACC for the name and phone number of the custodian at the hut. The Toronto Section contact information can be obtained through the national office in Canmore.

Hut fees per day are $7 for members and $10 for non-members. Season passes can be purchased for $60. Kids under 16 are free when accompanied by an adult member. Non-members must be accompanied by a member of the ACC.

The Keene Farm

HISTORY

The Keene property was purchased by the Montreal Section of the ACC in 1966 through the loans and donations of its members. The original farmhouse burned down in 1974 and was replaced two years later by the current structure. In 1989, a garage and workshop were built to house the tractor and tools.

LOCATION

General Location

The Keene Farm is located within the Adirondack Forest Preserve (State Park) in northern New York State, USA, approximately 50 km southwest of the city of Plattsburgh.

Amenities

Gas, groceries, shopping, and equipment are available in Keene, Keene Valley, and Lake Placid (all within 20 minutes by car). Montreal is a one hour and 45 minutes drive to the north.

Map Reference

USGS 7.5′ X 15′ Quadrangle – Lake Placid.

Grid Reference

The hut is located at 977057 on the above map of Lake Placid.

Altitude

The hut sits at 1,115 ft. (340m).

ACCESS

Approach

The Keene Farm is easily accessible from the Interstate #87 which runs north-south between Plattsburgh and Albany, NY.

Approaching from the south, take the 73 from Witherbee to Keene and the junction of the 9N. From the north, take exit 34 off the Interstate and follow the 9N from Keeseville to Jay and then to Upper Jay. The towns of Keene and Upper Jay are approximately 10 km apart on the 9N; the Keene Farm is just off Styles Brook Road, 5 km south of Upper Jay and five km north of the town of Keene. Once on the Styles Brook Road travel east 1.5 km to the gravel entrance to the property on the left. In the winter the gravel entrance may not be negotiable and it may be necessary to park on the side of the road and walk up to the hut.

FACILITIES

The Hut and Accommodation

The 103-acre property provides both camping facilities and a large cabin. There are many established camp sites with tables and fire pits in the meadows. Nearby is a large 30′ X 15′ open-sided shelter for cooking, eating, or escaping from inclement weather. The hut is a two-storey log structure on a small pine knoll overlooking the Ausable Valley. It has an entry and front porch, a large kitchen area, an eating/sitting room, and two large sleeping rooms upstairs with foam mattresses for 35 people.

Heat Source

Heating is provided by two wood-burning stoves. Wood is supplied at the hut year round.

Cooking

There are nine propane cooking elements in the kitchen area. Propane is supplied year round. There is a good selection of pots and pans, as well as eating utensils for about 20 people.

Lighting

Lighting for the hut is by propane lamps.

Water Supply

Water comes from an artesian well. The pump is located by the garage, about 30m from the hut. There is also a shallow well in the meadows.

Grey Water

Grey water is disposed of down the kitchen sinks.

Outhouses

There are three outhouses, one 15m from the hut and two others in the meadows.

Garbage

All garbage which cannot be burned in the fireplace must be packed out.

OPPORTUNITIES

Keene Farm is located in the heart of the High Peaks Region of the Adirondack Mountains. There are many nearby rock climbing areas and an extensive system of trails for day or multi-day trips. In the winter there is good ice climbing and winter mountaineering as well as downhill, backcountry and cross-country skiing on both natural trails and at track-set areas. Visitors should inquire locally about guide books for hiking, skiing and climbing.

RATES AND RESERVATIONS

If a member intends to bring more than five people, reservations must be made with the Keene Farm Manager. There are locks on the facility and the combination numbers are changed on a regular basis; the current number can be obtained from any Montreal Section Executive Member. You can get the Keene Farm Manager's phone number and address from the ACC National Office or by writing to:

Keene Farm Manager
Montreal Section ACC
P.O. Box 543
Victoria Station
Westmount, Quebec
H3Z 2V5

Overnight rates are as follows: Members of the Montreal Section stay at the hut for $7 per night, or camp for $5 per night. Non-members stay for $15 at the hut and camp for $7. Children (under 16) of members stay for free, and students (with ID) stay for half the regular rates.

Recommended Reading

Hiking:

Beers, Don. *Lake O'Hara Trails*. 1996

—— *Banff — Assiniboine: A Beautiful World*. 1993.

—— *The Wonder of Yoho*. 1989.

—— *The World of Lake Louise*. 1991.

Environment Canada. *Footloose in the Columbias — a hiker's guide to the trails of Mount Revelstoke and Glacier National Parks*. 1990.

Patton, Brian and Bart Robinson, *The Canadian Rockies Trail Guide,* Sixth Edition. 1994.

Potter, Mike. *Backcountry Banff*. 1992.

—— *Hiking Lake Louise, 2nd Edition*. 1994

Climbing:

Boles, Glen, et al. *Rocky Mountains of Canada — South*. 1979.

Dougherty, Sean. *Selected Alpine Climbs in the Canadian Rockies*. 1981.

Fox, Kevin, Roger Laurilla, et al. *The Columbia Mountains of Canada, Central*. 1992.

Martin, John and John Jones. *Sport Climbs in the Canadian Rockies,* 1996.

Josephson, Joe. *Waterfall Ice Climbs in the Canadian Rockies,* 3rd Edition. 1994.

—— Chris Perry and Andy Genereaux. *Ghost Rock* 1997.

Kane, Allan. *Scrambles in the Canadian Rockies*. 1992.

Kruszyna, Robert and William Putnam. *Rocky Mountains of Canada — North*. 1985.

Martin, John. *Kananaskis Rock*. 1989.

Perry, Chris, et al. *Bow Valley Rock*. 1988.

Skiing:

Daffern, Gillean. *Kananaskis Country Ski Trails*. 1992.

Daffern, Tony. *Avalanche Safety for Skiers and Climbers,* Second Edition. 1992.

Fredston, Jill and Doug Fesler. *Snow Sense*. 1994

Jamieson, Bruce and Torston Geldsetzer. *Avalanche Accidents in Canada*. 1996.

Scott, Chic. *Ski Trails in the Canadian Rockies*. 1992.

—— *Summits and Icefields*. 1994.

History and General Interest:

Engler, Bruno. *A Mountain Life: The Stories and Photographs of Bruno Engler* (R.W. Sandford, ed). 1996

Gadd, Ben. *Handbook of the Canadian Rockies,* Second Edition. 1995.

Morton, Keith. *Planning a Wilderness Trip in Canada and Alaska*. 1997

Mountaineers, The. *Mountaineering, the Freedom of the Hills,* 5th Edition. 1994.

Palmer, Howard. *Mountaineering and Exploration in the Selkirks*. 1914. (out of print)

Putnam, William, et al. *Placenames of the Canadian Alps*. 1991.

—— *The Great Glacier and Its House*. 1982.

Sanford, R.W.. *The Canadian Alps (The History of Mountaineering in Canada,* Volume 1). 1990.

Alpine Huts:

Alpine Club of Canada, The. *Water, Energy and Waste Management in Alpine Shelters Symposium: Notes from a Canadian Conference*. 1992.

Kariel, H. G. and P. E.. *Alpine Huts in the Rockies, Selkirks and Purcells*. 1986. (out of print)

Rollins, Jon and Charles Young. *An Inventory of Hut Sites in the Canadian Rockies and Northern Selkirks*. 1994.

Other Huts in the Area

Not all of the huts and backcountry shelters in the area are operated by the ACC. We often get phone calls asking for information about reserving huts which are operated by others; these are the most common:

Conrad Kain Hut — the Bugaboos

Location

The hut is near the Crescent Glacier in Bugaboo Glacier Provincial Park, B.C. It is an excellent base for the alpine rock climbing in the Bugaboos.

Operator

The hut is operated by B.C. Parks, East Kootenay District. For more information, call (250) 422-4200.

Reservations

It is not possible to make reservations for the Kain Hut — it is first-come-first-served for the 50 mattresses in the place. The rangers at the hut collect the fee.

Fees

The fee is $10 per person per night.

Facilities

The hut is well set up for cooking with a propane stove (propane supplied) and has foam mattresses for 50 people. The hut is also the location of the Bugaboo Ranger Station.

Naiset Cabins — Mt. Assiniboine

Location

The cabins are located on a bench above the east end of Lake Magog in Mt. Assiniboine Provincial Park.

Operator

The hut is operated by B.C. Parks, East Kootenay District. For more information, call (250) 422-4200.

Reservations

Reservations are mandatory in the winter (December 1st to May 31st), and will be accepted up to 30 days in advance. In the summer accommodation is on a first-come-first-served basis.

Fees

There is a $10 per person per night fee. In the winter this must be paid in advance at the time of reservation. In the summer the fees are collected by the rangers at Mt. Assiniboine Ranger Station.

Facilities

The cabins are each supplied with a small wood stove, a table and bunks for six to eight people. B.C. Parks requests that visitors bring in their own "Presto Logs" for heating.

R.C. Hind Hut — Mt. Assiniboine

Location

The hut is located above the headwall southwest of Lake Magog in Mt. Assiniboine Provincial Park.

Operator

The hut is operated by B.C. Parks, East Kootenay District. For more information, call (250) 422-4200.

Reservations

Accommodation is on a first-come-first-served basis.

Fees

There is no charge for staying at the Hind Hut.

Facilities

There are no facilities to speak of at the hut: no wood stove, no mattresses, no cooking or eating utensils. You're pretty much on your own.

Bryant Creek and Egypt Lake Shelters

Location

The Bryant Creek Shelter is northeast of Marvel Lake, on the trail to Mt. Assiniboine. The Egypt Lake Shelter is northeast of Egypt Lake. Both huts are in Banff National Park.

Operator

The huts are operated by Banff National Park.

Reservations

Reservations can be made up to 21 days in advance, and are made through Banff Park; call (403) 762-1550. Users may stay at the huts for no more than three consecutive nights.

Fees

There is no fee for staying at the hut; however, a backcountry permit is mandatory, and all overnight users in the backcountry must pay for a Wilderness Pass. The Wilderness Pass can be purchased at registration ($6 per person per night) or as a season's pass ($42).

Facilities

There are modest facilities at both huts. There is a wood-burning stove and a wood supply, however there are no sleeping mattresses or cooking and eating utensils.

Glacier Circle Hut

Location

The Glacier Circle Hut is located in Glacier Circle at the base of the Dawson Range, near the south end of the Illecillewaet Glacier, Glacier National Park, B.C.

Operator

The hut is operated by Glacier National Park.

Reservations

Reservations are made through Glacier National Park at Rogers Pass. The phone number is (250) 814-5232.

Fees

There is a $10 per person per night fee.

Facilities

The hut has a wood-burning stove, a Coleman stove and lanterns, cooking and eating utensils and foam mattresses.

Sapphire Col Hut

Location

The Sapphire Col Hut is located at Sapphire Col between the Dome and Mt. Jupiter, Glacier National Park, B.C.

Operator

The hut is operated by Glacier National Park.

Reservations

Reservations are made through Glacier National Park at Rogers Pass. The phone number is (250) 814-5232.

Fees

There is a $10 per person per night fee.

Facilities

The Sapphire Col Hut is a simple shelter for six people. There is no wood-burning stove, and the hut users are responsible for their own cook stove, utensils and mattresses.)

The Asulkan Cabin

Location

The Asulkan Cabin is located at the end of the Asulkan summer trail at an elevation of 2100 metres (grid reference MG 673737) in Glacier National Park, B.C.

Operator

The hut is operated by Glacier National Park.

Reservations

Reservations are made through the National Office of The Alpine Club of Canada. The phone number is (403) 678-3200.

Fees

There is a $20 per person per night fee.

Facilities

The Asulkan Cabin is equivalent to an ACC Class A hut. It has propane heating, lighting and cooking facilities, pots, pans and utensils, and sleeping foamies.

Important Phone Numbers

BOOKINGS

The Alpine Club of Canada
National Office, Hut and Clubhouse bookings
(403) 678-3200 (phone)
(403) 678-3224 (fax)

Canadian Alpine Centre and International Hostel at Lake Louise
(403) 522-2200 (phone)
(403) 522-2253 (fax)

Lake O'Hara
Bus (day use only)
(250) 343-6433

INFORMATION

Parks Canada Information

Banff Park
(403) 762-1550

Lake Louise Visitor's Centre
(403) 522-3833

Yoho Park
(250) 343-6783

Kootenay Park
(winter) (250) 347-9615
(summer) (250) 347-9505

Jasper Park
(403) 852-6176

Trail Information and Backcountry Reservations
(403) 852-6177

Glacier Park
(250) 814-5232

SAFETY

National Park Public Safety Wardens

Banff Park
(403) 762-1415

Lake Louise
(403) 522-3982

Jasper (24-hr emergency line)
(403) 852-6161

Jasper Warden Station
(403) 852-6156

Sunwapta Warden Station
(403) 852-5383

Yoho
(250) 343-6324

Kootenay
(250) 347-9361 or (250) 347-6371

Glacier
(250) 814-5202 or (250) 814-5212

Avalanche Conditions

Canadian Avalanche Association Recording
1-800-667-1105

Banff Avalanche Information
(403) 762-1460 (or call Parks Public Safety Offices)

Environment Canada Weather (Banff Area)
Recording (403) 762-2088

EMERGENCIES

Royal Canadian Mounted Police

Banff	(403) 762-2228
Canmore	(403) 678-5516
Field	(250) 343-6316
Golden	(250) 344-2221
Jasper	(403) 852-4421
Lake Louise	(403) 522-3811
Revelstoke	(250) 837-5255
Squamish	(604) 898-9611 (or 9-1-1)

Notes